IN THE
MOMENT

The process of training actors

JOE TURNER CANTÚ

In The Moment The Process of Training Actors © copyright, 2015, Joe Turner Cantú. All rights reserved. No part of this book may be reproduced without the express, written consent of the publisher except in the case of brief quotations embodied in critical articles and reviews.

For information contact: Nautilus Publishing,
426 South Lamar Blvd., Suite 16, Oxford, MS 38655.

ISBN: 978-1-93694661-7

The Nautilus Publishing Company
426 South Lamar Blvd., Suite 16
Oxford, Mississippi 38655
Tel: 662-513-0159
www.nautiluspublishing.com

First Edition

Cover photo: ThinkStock by GettyImages
Author photo: Jenny Kate Luster

Library of Congress Cataloging-in-Publication Data has been applied for.

Printed in the USA

10   9   8   7   6   5   4   3   2   1

For Eddie, Mary Frances,
and my Family

Contents

INTRODUCTION

"I think I love and reverence all arts equally, only putting my own just above others; because in it I recognize the union and culmination of my own. To me it seems as if when God conceived the world, that was Poetry; He formed it, and that was Sculpture; He colored it, and that was Painting; He peopled it with living beings, and that was the grand, divine, eternal Drama."

—*Charlotte Cushman 1816-1876 (on acting)*

As a teenager, the words of Charlotte Cushman, the celebrated nineteenth century actress, inspired me to dream; they also gave me a framework by which to approach "this drama thing" that I was gradually and methodically coming to understand. It was a thing that I had dreamt of doing, but never dared think of in terms of actually doing. It was impractical, albeit fun, fluff, like most of the arts; that is what I thought I had learned from school and community, and thought to be general consensus. I took it to be truth. Later I discovered that I had been operating on a false assumption. The opposite was true; my Texan-American upbringing demonstrated that the arts could be a haven, a place to unload, a place to express, a home that sheltered me from the fears of growing up. The false assumption had been based on "common knowledge," which did not consider innate talent or personal interest. In sharp contrast, popular culture was a veritable deluge of TV and big-screen images, pumping images of actors into my psyche, forcing me to take notice of the actors' work. While observing the actors, especially the child actors, the thought – *I can do that* – increasingly popped up. But the reality of doing it was prevented by something I knew all too well as a child: fear.

I soon learned that I was going to have to come to terms with fear as both foe and friend, as confidante, as obstacle, as process. Framing fear as each of these (confidante, obstacle, process) and dealing with it in each context sequentially helped shape my personal understanding of what it meant to act or to be an actor. I had to define all the parts of what it was to act on stage, as opposed to acting up, acting out, or simply putting on an act, which are the terms that early on were obstacles for the very naïve, young actor that I was – the young actor that, thank God, still exists somewhere inside. I am thankful to be directly connected to the process that I, as a young actor, journeyed, on the way to answering the questions that others did not, or could not, answer, whether they were peer, director, coach, or teacher.

What I do know is that I learn more about acting every day; I'm thankful it never ends. As is the case with most knowledge, I've learned more about acting since I've been teaching it these past three decades. Yes, I was a good actor, a damn good actor. No, I don't act much anymore, not since I lost my "actor's ego" two decades ago. Do I have to remain an active actor in order to be a good acting teacher? No. Teaching acting is its very own art form and craft. I'm sure most of you would agree that acting is not a hobby; well, neither is the teaching of it. It takes professionals to impart any and all knowledge. But if you want to be a great or effective teacher of acting, you will be, as long as you keep your ego at bay, and keep your actors' well-being at the forefront of every day's work.

The intent of this book, or manual, is to provide you an opportunity to view the training of actors through the mind and heart of the actor trainer, and, simultaneously through the eyes of the actor, as she or he experiences the tangible and intangible intricacies, techniques, and impulses that literally play into what most people see as a final product. Most of this, you might say, you already know, due to years of study, experience, and common sense. My hope is that you find at least one new approach to extracting pathos and believability from your actors, be it in a production of a play, a directorial coaching session on the sound stage, or a class in the studio.

I hope you find this book to be a practical guide or reference.

PART I
Internal Process

1

UNDERSTANDING AND PREPARING THE NOVICE ACTOR: FRIENDLY FEAR

Everyone acts on some level, but few people act with a conscious purpose in mind. You might say that everyone who acts on some level is merely *re*acting to the moment at hand. The job of instructing someone interested in acting on stage or for the camera is left to acting teachers, coaches, director/coaches, and the actor. People who have little working knowledge about theatre or the entertainment industry might not appreciate the rigorous process of training actors. Actors, directors, choreographers, and teachers appreciate the process because they have come to respect it, due mainly to the many hours, days, and years of disciplined work and sharp focus.

The term *novice actor* refers to anyone who is new to the art or business of *acting*, whatever the age. Since acting is both an art form and a hard and fast business, it must be said that sometimes, when training an actor, we are training the artist, and sometimes we are training a person who will be pursuing a place in the industry; and, oftentimes, we are training both. It matters not the age of the actor in training; high school students need information about the art and the business (or *industry*) as much as actors in college or graduate programs, conservatories, or professional schools. The point is to always be clear about the art form when addressing (or *teaching*) the art form and the business when referring to the business. These are two separate yet equal aspects of the "art of acting." True; one cannot exist without the other. Every actor needs to understand the art as well as the etiquette, generally-accepted vocabulary, and the business that is a part of the professional trade or community theater. I refer to the business of acting often. When I speak of it, I am speaking of the physical application of the business of acting and the task of mounting and producing theatre or a role in a scripted work. This I see as separate, though both exist simultaneously and inter-dependently. An easy way of differentiating between the two can come down to the difference between *theatre* and *theater*, "*re*" being the art form, and "*er*" representing the building, venue, or working space.

You are now in your studio space and an actor stands before you, thinking or saying, essentially: *I'm all yours. Work your magic.* This is the case if the actor has been around a block or two, and feels comfortable with the art and possibly the business, as well. This actor we will address in upcoming sections and chapters.

When a young, or novice, actor stands before you, ready for work, the first question on his or her mind is: *Am I going to make a fool of myself?* The second thought is: *How will I remember my lines?* From the outset, these two fears must either be addressed or dispelled. The answer to the first question is: *Yes, you must be willing to risk being a fool because sooner or later, it will happen.* Done. And, if they reject the notion of risking being a fool, you have your first clue that this person might not be suited for this art form or business. *Taking oneself too seriously is an obstacle that can be addressed; genuinely wanting to be sincere is not an obstacle at all.* As for memorization, I prefer not to address it all, until it becomes an issue, or to never use the word *memorize*, which tends to paralyze a sector of the brain for some reason. I prefer to use the old-fashioned term "*learning lines by heart.*" Your working process should begin with exercises that tap into the actor's inner world and not tie up the actor's brain with the memorization of lines. Descriptions of such exercises, like the personal monologue, will follow.

You would have a valid argument if you pointed out that young actors who do not learn how to memorize by rote might never achieve self-confidence. I would argue that the actual novice process of memorization is too mercurial. Most young actors learn lines through repetition, which in and of itself is good. But are they learning words, or thoughts and deeds? You want them, from the outset, to learn how to "memorize" all while absorbing or breathing in the thought, the objective, the complex human moment. That is why I merely avoid this by pretending that the mental process will take care of itself if our task at hand focuses on the intention or the action which happens to come wrapped in words or, at times, silence. Understanding intentions will lead to clarity and, quite often, movement, however stiff. Young actors, particularly, must be encouraged to move, to take action. If not, the tendency will be to simply attempt to feel or force an emotion— not a good thing.

Never encourage your young (or novice) actor to feel; simply have them create the environment in which they will take action. Emotions in young actors are as hit-or-miss as slot machines; you never know from moment to moment whether you'll get lemons or cherries. The goal is to create what Constantin Stanislavski called *given circumstances*, in an effort to identify and achieve "believable truth." The given circumstances are exactly that, the circumstances that lead the character to the moment at hand. Focus on these and you and your actor will always succeed on some level.

Another common challenge, primarily with young actors, is physical stiffness. The stiffness in young actors is not merely a result of being a newcomer to the art form; it is a direct symptom of the brain's doing most of the work. *This probably sounds wrong to many of you, given the fact that we cannot function without the brain.* Granted, it is a physiological fact that the brain controls our involuntary and voluntary impulses and vital functions. However, for an actor, the thinking brain can sometimes become more of an obstacle as the actor progresses in her training toward *characterization* (creating the character) or playing the *moment* (reacting in the here and now.) So, am I suggesting that we ignore the brain functions?

Yes. Or rather, I am suggesting that we not dwell on the brain functions. Note that most of your actors are highly intuitive and/or intelligent people. You don't need to further intellectualize something that most of them have thought entirely too much about. *Factual analysis is excellent; self-analysis is not where you want to begin.* In the early lessons, the young (or novice) actor needs to be discouraged from excessive complex thought and, rather, be encouraged to experience each present moment.

THE PERSONAL MONOLOGUE

The easiest, most efficient way to cut through many initial acting obstacles is to have the actor prepare and present (not perform) (*note the purposeful use of vocabulary*), a personal monologue.

A personal monologue is exactly what it implies. It is a 3 to 5 minute story, or monologue, that the actor personally experienced at some point in his or her life. It needn't be tragic or comedic, though most choose to share something funny that happened on their favorite vacation, for example. Surprisingly, several actors may choose to use this exercise to open up to their peers and to you; they instinctively take the opportunity to explore their inner landscape.

The *directions* should be simple and specific: "Choose a personal incident from your life experience and talk about it to the class, using notes of your choice. Order of presentation will be drawn today."

The personal monologue is, of course, an ice-breaker that achieves several goals simultaneously. Firstly, the group gets to know each other. Also, the actors get to present in front of an audience without feeling like they are performing. And they are speaking their very own language or words, however they want. The personal monologue also begins to validate their personal experiences as important – to themselves and to others.

Most of the actors will use note cards or a sheet of paper. Some will write out every word of their monologue and will want to read it. Some will *ad lib* their experience. And a select few will choose to *perform* their personal monologue – taking on the role of a character; these are the very students who desperately need this exercise and should be asked to not *act* the monologue, but simply to share the experience. "I thought this was an acting class," they might say. The response is simple: "The objective of this exercise is to share, not to perform. Don't worry; there will be plenty of time devoted to performing. Now, please put the paper down and just share the experience. We are all here supporting you and we care to know what happens when you are just yourself." The moment after sharing their personal monologue, this actor will have taken the first step toward making friends with *fear*.

How can the actor turn the obstacle of fear into his confidante? How best to use it as a personal motivator? These are two of the best questions we as actor-trainers need to ask ourselves throughout most of the early process because it is by answering these vital questions that we come to terms with the specific needs of each individual. By answering these questions, we have begun the process of genuinely training these actors. Notice that we are not concentrating on any particular method here; we are simply beginning the journey through a psychological landscape. The destination is the same but the route is unique for each individual. This will become clearer when we work through the process monologue, a highly structured yet flexible exercise designed to address and confront personal obstacles.

MOVEMENT AND MENTAL RELEASE
THROUGH THEATRE GAMES

Novice actors need to move, especially the young ones. They immediately ease up and open out physically and vocally when they are moving. Any physical and vocal warm-up is good, but the best work at this point is theatre games. The improvisation-based games made famous by Viola Spolin are still the best because they demand play. Young actors know the value of playing even if they don't easily connect with it; older novice actors quickly find that the *playing* through improvisational games leads them to that place of release. Again, should one of the actors be uncomfortable with improvisation games, this is a clear indication to you that they will need to confront this sooner or later. It very likely goes back to not wanting to make a fool of themselves.

One solid theatre game or physical exercise is all you need to get them breathing, and at this point you will see their bodies release and their faces open up and out. This is the perfect time to have them spontaneously repeat sections of their personal monologue from wherever they are. Follow this with another 30-second physical exercise, followed by one or two more sections of their personal monologues (one at a time.) Go through the entire group, having each of them share a 20-second portion of their story soon after they are breathing heavily from the physical exercise. The idea is to catch their bodies "off guard" while they are in the *playing* mode. The results will encourage and possibly surprise you, but more importantly, your actors will thank you. When they thank you after an exercise, you should always acknowledge that something has happened experientially that they instinctively understand, even if they cannot yet verbalize it. They are making the transition from thinking about how to act to re-experiencing a moment in their narrative.

SCRIPT ANALYSIS

Soon after you feel the actors have gotten a taste of acting in the moment via movement or play during their personal monologues, it is time for them to learn how to articulate their observations when reading a script. They very likely have come to you with a keen eye for visual observation (although this can always improve), but it is the act of articulating their observations on paper that will bring about fundamental, lasting knowledge of a character and the character's journey within a story. At this point, you might be wondering: Why analyze anything when you are still in an exploratory, early stage? And you should pat yourself on the back for asking an excellent question. Whether research scientists agree or disagree about the concrete versus the creative "sides" of the brain, left and right hemispheres specifically, my decades of experience point to the fact that you must exercise the concrete alongside the creative for best, and, yes, lasting results when learning anything new. Understanding character personality traits and what that character will face enables an actor to make informed moment-to-moment decisions about their intention and motivations.

There are five components to the basic analysis of any theatrical work: 1) synopsis; 2) character breakdown; 3) plot structure breakdown or analysis; 4) scholarly criticism or reviews; and 5) a personal response. When an actor can provide all five, you can trust that they will always pay attention to the details when they are confronted with future reading of scripts for character research and/or role preparation.

The synopsis needs to be brief; a short paragraph is best. The character breakdown of principal characters needs to answer at a glance who, what, when, and where. Oedipus is a king from Thebes in ancient Greece, married with children, concerned about a prophecy. The plot structure analysis needs to reveal where in the play we can find exposition, conflict introduction, rising action, complications, rising action, climax, and resolution. The actor should produce at least three quotes from published criticism and/or reviews. And she must provide a brief personal reaction to the play.

Here is a sample entry from my college undergraduate Beginning Acting syllabus:

SCRIPT ANALYSIS: 3 PLAYS

You must choose three plays to analyze: a Greek Classic *from the required textbook anthology*, an Early or Mid-Twentieth Century Drama *from the required textbook anthology* and an Ethnic or Non-traditional Contemporary play (with professor's approval) or Contemporary Drama *from the required textbook anthology*. Write a minimum 5-page **type-written paper, 12 point Arial font, double-spaced**, containing: 1) <u>synopsis</u>; 2) <u>character breakdowns</u>; 3) <u>plot structure analysis</u>; 4) <u>a one-page list of published dramatic criticism or scholarly reviews of the play, minimum of three quoted sources</u>; and a 5) <u>personal reaction to the analysis of the play</u>. You will also prepare a **5-minute** (timed) **oral report** based on your analysis of the play. You will need to turn in your paper when you deliver your oral presentation. <u>You may not do your oral presentation unless you are also turning in your paper.</u> *Class will complete their presentations for Greek before presenting on 20th Century, etc.* Five points off if you do not present when scheduled. (Wednesday, September 26 – Friday, October 19.) *You will draw for order of presentation on the day you receive your Script Analysis study guides, approximately two weeks prior to start of unit work. 30% of course grade.*

The best actors learn early on how to analyze a script as they read. This skill will serve them during their pivotal training years, and will be crucial for professional auditions. Most audition callbacks include cold readings from "sides" (sections of the script) selected for the casting of specific roles. The actors are handed the sides and are then given a few minutes to look them over prior to auditioning. From the moment the actors are given the sides, they must make bold choices based on what they know about the character, from prior reading or just from the side itself (if it is a new work). Their ability, as actors, to observe the word on page (*text*) and interpret it creatively using personal and appropriate mannerisms will get them the role or keep their audition fresh in the auditor's mind for future casting.

AUDITIONING IN BEGINNING CLASSES

No acting class is complete without at least one unit of work on or including the auditioning process. The best gift you can give your novice actors is to provide them the opportunity of practice auditions at least once a year. Young or novice actors do not come to you with substantial experience; you need to provide it. Remind yourself often that even the gifted actors must impress the director or casting director in the initial and callback audition if they are to be cast. They will not be cast on your recommendation alone. I include audition material suggestions that pertain to specific topics, depending on the subject matter, throughout the book.

Prepare your actors for the general audition or "cattle call." The general audition, most of the time, is a 1-minute monologue that gives the auditors an opportunity to decide whether or not to ask the actor back for a callback audition. Time their audition with a stopwatch. Have them "slate": state their name and number prior to the audition and repeat their name and number after their 1-minute audition, preferably with a smile. Have the actors dress nicely but comfortably in clothing that represents them as individuals for this practice audition. Far too often, actors shoot themselves in the foot by looking less than "respectful" for the general audition. Remind them that first impressions are usually lasting.

Trusting our intuition as artists is the key ingredient, if you will, in most anything we form, shape, or create – anything we do.

BASIC MONOLOGUE WORK

All of the theatre games up to this point and any audition experience have enhanced the actors' understanding of how to respond impulsively to a situation or moment. It is time to dissect the acting of a non-personal monologue, which will, in turn, improve the actors' auditioning skills.

Words and actions must be clear and moment-specific is your mantra with monologue material. Of course, it can remain your mantra throughout the training process, but it is especially valuable as you draw out the student as either *an actor* or as *the character* (sometimes, but not always, the same). When you ask a question, be clear about whom you are addressing: the actor, or the character. Should you ask the character a question, expect the character to answer and expect to use the character's name when addressing the person in front of you.

Acting coach: *How are you feeling at this moment?*

Actor: *Who me, Patrick, or Willy Loman, the character?*

Choose and you're off and running. And remain true to each moment. Feel free to cross back to speaking with the actor after speaking with the character, but finish the specific moment, or answer the question; accomplish the goal at hand before switching.

Actors enjoy answering questions about themselves, but they might find answering questions as the character a bit difficult if they do not know enough about the character. That is why the script analysis exercise, resulting in some kind of character profile, is always helpful to both of you. Ask them for at least a one-page paper that details aspects of the character, based on having read the entire script. (*See Chapter Twelve, *The Character Profile Paper,* for details.)

Once you have asked the actor or character pertinent questions, and feel satisfied with the answers, go immediately to the actions demanded by the text. Ask the actor to *present* (not *act*) the monologue, using the actions prescribed by the text. Should the monologue, like most, be primarily a heartfelt first-person account of an incident or memory, ask the actor, as an exercise, to create an activity that might accompany the monologue. If the actor cannot concoct an activity, then give them an activity to accompany the communication of the monologue. Any activity that engages their mind and body will do, even if it appears nonsensical. Remember, you want them to communicate with their entire being, not just their mind and mouth. Eventually they will find their way to an honest full-body communication of the monologue.

Once you feel they have spoken the monologue in an honest, full-bodied manner, work with them on *target focus*. Target focus is what dancers call *spotting*, especially when doing a pirouette. I add the word *target* to emphasize the need for the audience to know who the character is addressing. Is the character addressing one imaginary person? Is the character addressing the audience? Is the character addressing two people? If so, where are they? If the character is addressing one person, does the person move in the course of the monologue? In other words, does the *target* move? I know that for most acting teachers and coaches, the word *focus* encompasses all this. I have found that by using the term target focus, the actor knows specifically what I am referring to. By answering these questions and helping the actor to visualize these details, you and the actor will accomplish the ultimate goal: to stimulate the audience's imagination.

Suspended disbelief is an acting, or theatre, term that describes what the audience experiences when expected to believe something that is not *concrete* or *real*. For example, a character is describing the snowfall, maybe even feeling the snowflakes on her tongue or face. Though we in the audience might not see actual snowflakes falling onstage we "suspend our disbelief" and go along for the ride. This is the *magic* of theatre.

The ultimate goal of an actor performing a monologue is for the audience to believe every word, every image, and every action.

Here is a sample entry from my college undergraduate Beginning Acting syllabus:

2-MINUTE ACTIVITY/CONTEMPORARY MONOLOGUE

The student actor must choose a new contemporary monologue from a produced play or screenplay. *Two minutes in length.* (It will be timed, so cut the monologue to two minutes.) **A Character Profile paper will be due on the day of first round presentation and due completed for second round presentation.** An activity, the language and character and its relationship to you will be explored in this unit of work. *The two goals of this unit of work are clarity and specificity.* (Round One, Round Two notes and a Final Round. Five points off if you do not present when scheduled. Monday, August 27 – Monday, September 24.) *Schedule will be distributed prior to first working day; order of presentation opposite of Personal Monologue order.* 20% of course grade.

SCENEWORK

Actors audition alone during the general audition or "cattle call," but they act, most of the time, with others. Performing a scene allows you and them the opportunity to work on *listening* and *responding*, the two most important components when performing a role in a scene (play, screenplay, or television script.) Encourage both actors in the preferably two-person scene to allow for each other's impulses to inform the scene, the language, and each other. True exploration is critical at the beginning stages of scenework, prior to the actors' tendency to "make tapes."

"Making tapes" is when the actors glue themselves to one way of speaking or moving or intoning the lines and character. It will sound or look stiff and "put on." These are habits that the young actors learned from having to teach themselves for the most part, or from being forced to produce caricatures prior to understanding *character.* Do your best to have them speak as themselves and encourage them to use the same speaking voice that they use in everyday conversation. Encourage them to speak as if they were still working on honest impulse work. Discourage any attempt to create character if one of your actors "makes tapes."

Next, work with both actors on their:

1) **General focus**: Does their eye contact match the demands of the

text? Are they truly listening to their scene partner, listening with their eyes, not just ears? Is their focus giving the audience clues regarding the moments?

2) **Timing**: Are they speaking the language in a moment-to-moment appropriate manner, as opposed to speaking in a monotone, for example? Is the timing of the scene building and/or appropriately fluctuating, thereby reflecting the actions the characters engage themselves and each other in?

3) **Physicality**: Are the actors using their bodies to express themselves? Or are they acting from the neck up?

4) **Creating and responding to the environment**: Are they creating appropriate "fourth wall" imagery? (The fourth wall is the imaginary space between the actor and the audience, reflected in the actor's body language. *Do you believe the character is looking out a window?*) Are the actors responding to their environment? *Cold? Hot? Office chaos? Summer breeze? Rain? Pounding roof? Etc.*

5) Finally, go back to the first step. Are the actors **listening** and **responding** to each other? Are the characters listening and responding to each other?

By the time you have engaged the actors in all this work, you can rest assured they have made friends with fear. They are now ready to address and confront personal obstacles.

•••

They will feel like old pros, ready for anything.

2

THE PROCESS MONOLOGUE:
ADDRESSING AND CONFRONTING OBSTACLES

The ability to *access* and *share* an *honest impulse* lies at the heart of the art of acting. Your actors have, indeed, been required to access honest impulses during their improvisation exercises and theatre games and scenework; they also access impulses every waking moment of their lives and share these impulses when interacting with others. So, this is not some difficult aspect of the art of acting that deserves anything more than a "how-to" explanation. What exactly is an honest impulse? The *honest impulse* is an organic, immediate moment (or event) characterized by a wholly integrated, specifically singular, and clear action.

HONEST IMPULSES

The key to guiding your actors to recognize, access, then choose to share an *honest impulse* is to always remain clear with them about every moment and demand clarity and specificity of yourself and them. You cannot demand anything of actors that you are not willing to uphold. In other words, do not inadvertently trick your actors. For example, this would not be a good time to use sarcasm or to be cynical regarding any aspects of their work. When they see that you are genuinely remaining true to the goal or process you have presented, and when they sense that you respect them, they will, in turn, trust you and follow your lead. Then you will be in place to encourage the sharing of their impulses, which will come in the form of: a smile, a genuine gesture, a fidgety leg, a look, a habitual sound, a nervous tick, a response to you or a fellow actor …and the list can go on. Remember that simplification is the "magic" when training actors.

An *impulsive* sound, word, gesture, or movement happens only when we are not *thinking* of any end result or finished product. The moment any human being engages in action with an end result in mind, the road to that end result is not impulsive and is questionably honest. It is very important that you, as the actor's guide, insist on honest impulses: honest answers, honest sounds, honest gestures, and honest movements. So, you might ask, *"What is a dishonest impulse? How can I possibly know what is truly honest and what is a lie?"*

Is the actor's nervous leg bouncing up and down honest? Yes, and what is that leg saying to you? Is the avoidance of eye contact with you an honest impulse? Yes, and what is the avoidance saying to you? Is the forced laughter an honest impulse? No, and what does that say to you? These behaviors give you insight into what an actor is struggling with, what they keep hidden, and what they feel self-conscious about.

THE PROCESS MONOLOGUE

The process monologue is a useful tool that helps reveal internal psychological (and physical) defenses that would lead an actor to obfuscate an honest emotion. The actor selects a 2-3-minute monologue from a current or contemporary play that they have not previously worked on and presents the memorized monologue to the class as best they can. The monologue must be serious in purpose and dramatic in genre. Why? Because the work that we will be doing is serious in purpose, and comedy (however difficult comedy truly is) does not lend itself to getting past, or through, personal obstacles. Oftentimes, the obstacles themselves are what allow an actor to be impulsively and genuinely funny, at which time the obstacles become actor's tools. I often refer to this journey of exploration and discovery as the process monologue map. When I sit down to work with an actor on his or her process monologue, I have no idea, prior to starting, where the journey will lead. But I do know one thing: the actor is going to lead me. She will show me the way. His tight voice, due to throat tension, will lead me. Her nervous giggle will lead me. His downward-turned pursed lips will lead me. Her tilted sitting position will lead me. His perfectly spoken and perfectly "acted" process monologue, when presented for the first time, will lead me.

The actor stands or sits in front of you and the group of fellow actors. **First**, they present their memorized monologue as best they can. When they have finished presenting their monologue, they sit down in front of you and the group of fellow actors. The number one rule of this process is that only you can speak to the actor during the bulk of this process; toward the end of the process there will easily be time for the fellow actors to offer comments, but they must be filtered by you, depending on how deeply the work touches places of vulnerability with the actor. Remember that you are asking the actor to trust you with his or her essence. Yes, *essence*. How do you think actors *become* characters? It's not by accident; or if it is by accident alone, it will certainly not be consistent and never *great*. There is no understating the importance of this. The moment we make this process something less than what it truly is, we are essentially minimizing the power and purpose of the human being sitting in front of us. It is imperative to provide a psychologically safe environment for the actor to strip away their self-consciousness and reveal their most private selves.

Secondly, the tedious process of asking questions and gently but firmly encouraging answers may go something like this: **Asking the actor:** Why did you choose this monologue? What is the character talking about? Why do you believe the character is saying what she says? Do you like the character? **Asking the character:** Where are you from? Are you serious about what you just said? Why? What do you really mean? Who are you talking to? Do you expect them to believe you? Does it matter? Why? **Asking the actor:** Your voice is cracking. Why? You say your left leg is feeling a bit numb, why do you think that is? Circulation Is it just a physical occurrence? Have you ever lied to anyone? (At this moment, with this type of question, you have crossed a threshold; you are beginning to question the actor's purpose. And the actor will not like this at all; should they recognize this, some actors will cover up the uncomfortable feelings with humor or laughter. You must persist through it all, all the while being ever so careful to keep the actor's best interest in mind. Remember, you are on a mission. Like a good archeologist, you are searching for obstacles.) You continue: Are you lying to us now or are you telling us the truth? Is the character telling the truth? And so on and on you go, back and forth between the character and the actor until you get to the place of sheer honesty, a place of purity. That place might be bashful, beaming shyness, or it might be tears. It might be genuine laughter. But if it is laughter, it will not be the laughter of avoidance; it will be laughter from the gut that is a whole, full-bodied expression.

Thirdly, when you have reached that honest, pure place with the actor, you must begin to identify and address one or two of the actor's obstacles. This involves delicately confronting the actor about the obstacles. How you do this is the most complex part of this work because your intuition must inform you at this time. Common sense must be your guide, as your intuition informs you. Yes, you have already begun to confront the obstacles by challenging the actor with questions like, "Are you lying to us now?" But you have yet to ask the actor directly about the obstacle(s).

The obstacle might be a feeling of genuine shame or embarassment due to empathizing with the character's dilemma. The obstacle could be habitual shortness of breath when nervous. The obstacle might reveal an inability to compromise with authority figures.

Ask her why she needs that obstacle. Ask him the purpose of the obstacle. Ask her how and how long the obstacle has served her. Ask him the same question. Ask him if he needs that obstacle in order to present or perform his monologue. Ask her if the obstacle is something that she needs in order to perform a scene with a fellow actor. The actors will guide you with their answers. If they trust you, they will be forthcoming. If they do not trust you (or anyone else, for that matter), you will need to confront them with the obstacle that is *being mistrustful* of others. You will eventually get to the heart of the matter(s) and you will then need to provide them personal assignments after they speak the monologue again.

Ask them to speak a portion of the monologue to one of the fellow actors in the room. This will be very telling. Most of the time, you and the group will notice a marked difference in the delivery or presentation. Congratulate them on being able to speak the monologue simply and honestly.

Before you let them off the hook, as I just mentioned, you must give them an assignment or two. The **assignments** can range from telling a joke every day to a fellow actor to sharing a personal matter (that can be shared) with a fellow actor every day or once a week. The assignment could be making a list of all their excellent qualities. The assignment could be presenting the monologue again without the nervous knee bouncing. It all depends on what specifically you both have uncovered. The assignments should serve to reinforce the eventual demolition of the obstacle(s). For example, if Jason's first obstacle to tackle is to stop that nervous leg bouncing, he might need to journal every occurrence of leg-bouncing for the next week; if Sally's first obstacle to tackle is to stop gazing up and over someone's shoulder when she is communicating something honestly, she might need to journal looking people in the eye every time she speaks to someone.

Since your goal is to help them become better actors, it is also important that you find a way back to the character, not just as a short exercise but as a major portion of the process monologue work. Actors need to be reminded that all this work is not just about them; it's about the character they are currently addressing, the characters they will encounter in the future. When you ask them to present the monologue yet again (whether it is the same day or another) do it with one goal in mind: *truthful communication via the character.* Yes, you have worked on personal honesty, honest impulses, and reducing the number of obstacles, but the reason you've done this work is to allow a clear and simple pathway for the character to travel, to reside in, to express, to function. ***The character must have free, unlimited access to the actor's mind, body and psyche.*** It is not the actor who is "putting on" the character as if the character were a costume or a mask; even mask work is not about "putting on" anything, it is all about *freeing, giving over to* the "character."

Here is a sample entry from my college undergraduate BFA Acting syllabus:

PROCESS MONOLOGUE

Choose a new Contemporary monologue (*serious in purpose; dramatic genre*) from a produced play that is accessible to read thoroughly; meaning you must read the entire script prior to presenting it. ***Two to Three minutes (max.) in length***. A Character Profile paper will be due on the day of first and second round presentations. The language and character and its relationship to you will be explored briefly in the first round of work; the bulk of the work will be a personally guided process regarding effective, open communication and recognition of obstacles. This is a very important unit of work, so choose a monologue with which you easily connect. *Honest communication is the goal of this unit of work*. Round One, Round Two notes and a Final Round. Tuesday, August 28 – Tuesday, October 2. *Order of presentation is opposite of Lip-Sync order*. 20% of course grade.

The second time the actors present their process monologue, (in a week or two), ask each of them for a minimum of a one-page paper that details aspects of the character, based on having read the entire script. (*See Chapter Twelve, *The Character Profile Paper* for details.) The goals for this second go-round, or as I choose to call it, the *second round*, should relate to the assignments you gave them the day they first presented their process monologue. It would also be helpful to begin to include vocal goals, speech or diction goals, and movement or physicality goals. Include them as secondary but include them nonetheless, to remind them that they will be focusing more and more on the technical, skill-oriented, aspects of acting, as the months and years role by.

You will be able to measure your success with this important unit of work by observing the characters that your actors have created. Do you believe what the character is saying and doing? Or is too much of the actor still getting in the way? These are your measuring questions. Please do not hesitate to evaluate your actors, specific to the task at hand. Why do I ask you to evaluate them? Because if they are serious about training for the profession, they must prepare for a profession that is all about measuring up to someone's standards. Remember that a vital part of training actors is to prepare them for a profession that expects much and offers little in terms of generous encouragement. Please, do encourage each of them, as individuals and as a group. They expect and, at times, demand your encouragement, as well they should. But do also be clear about the meaning behind the pat on the back. Let them know the pat on the back is for the work they just completed and not about their entire career, which they have not completed. Utilize the psychology of achieving one goal at a time, one solid accomplishment after another.

There is an anecdote about Christopher Reeve, the late actor who was best known for his portrayal of Superman on the big screen, that may or may not be true but is most certainly popular among "theatre people." When Christopher Reeve was a young, recently-trained actor, he always looked forward to his nineteenth audition. He did anything he could to get to that nineteenth audition, never worrying about the one at hand, because he knew the nineteenth would bring him work. He never, ever, reached a nineteenth audition, always getting work long before the fifth, the tenth or the twelfth.

•••

One well-executed goal at a time – this is what your actors must learn in order to survive, and certainly to succeed.

3

BREATH, MOVEMENT, AND APPLICATION

The beginning exercises and the process monologue method cannot begin to develop the student's acting sensibilities and instincts without the proper use of **breath**. We all know or recognize the need for breath when conducting any activity, from reading quietly to running a marathon. And we do take it for granted most of the time because, *thank God*, it is an involuntary function; we don't have to think about it in order for the life-sustaining breathing process to occur. But we do have to think about it when we are re-ordering, or adjusting our habitual use, or mis-use, of breath. Without proper use of breath the actor cannot access vocal, physical, and mental nuance or power. From the miniscule moment in a scene to that climactic sword fight or speech, it is the use of breath (the body's fuel), that measures the effectiveness of the actor's work.

For actors, generally speaking, it is best to engage in some type of physical activity or sport so that breathing deeply and efficiently becomes a habit. In addition, the actor must learn how to use or manipulate her breath to create different theatrical effects. The breath directly affects qualities of the voice. This becomes most apparent when performing a highly physical scene; we may reach a certain limit at which speech becomes difficult. The physical demands of a scene make us well aware when we reach a certain physical limit; when this happens there is a direct relationship to the breath. What is less obvious is the fact that breath greatly influences our thinking process. Rapid shallow breaths exacerbate anxiety and fright, and deep, slow breaths are calming and relaxing (possibly due to changes in the balance of oxygen and carbon dioxide in our bodies).

You probably have experienced the exhilaration of the moment when your novice actor begins to make the mind/body connection that is critical to optimizing creative expression. Why did your actors make that brilliant discovery at the tail end of that arduous late evening rehearsal? They were at the point of exhaustion. They were no longer using their thinking brain to control the delivery of their lines. Their nerves were frayed. They wanted to "get it done and go home." As they quit thinking their way through they allowed their bodies (and breath) to take over for them. And they weren't shocked by what brilliance felt like, they simply loved the feeling; what did surprise them was the ease with which "it just happened." This was immediately followed by their question: *Why can't it always happen like this?* Your answer: *It can and it will, every time you allow your body and breath to lead the way.*

It's no surprise that breath/body/mind connections reside at the heart of acting excellence. It is also not surprising that we tend to resist giving over control to anything other than our keen minds. Our minds sharpen our creativity, keep us organized and upright, guard us from possible danger, monitor our body functions; of course we resist "giving over" to breath and physicality and chance. You, however, must understand and appreciate this conundrum, all while encouraging your actors to "let go."

Encourage your actors to trust their breath. And discourage them from becoming too dependent on you. When they find themselves lost, or adrift in a momentary lack of confidence, train them to focus on taking full belly breaths to quiet their anxious minds. It is difficult enough for young actors, novice actors, and all actors, for that matter, to accept the amount of rejection that accompanies a career in acting. Success will come their way, especially if they define success for themselves, and do not allow the industry or you to define it for them. Something as seemingly intangible as breath and meditation can turn out to be a solace, a friend, and a nurturing support as time goes by.

When training your actors to use breath properly throughout their work, the end product (or performance) cannot be the goal. You, as the monitor, need to remain disconnected on some level from the end product in order to continually monitor their breath. *Why?* Because if the actor is to allow the breath to flow, with the goal of surrendering himself to it, he cannot be expected to simultaneously monitor it, so it becomes your job. *The better you get at observing the human breath, the better a trainer, coach, and director you will become.* This is another secret to becoming a "good acting teacher" or "great director." Audiences remember being moved by the human beings on that stage; yes, they appreciate great sets and costumes, but they know that the performances determine the greatness of the piece of work. Audiences are very smart. And they want to be taken on a ride; they have paid to be taken on that ride. After the brilliance of lighting, scenic technology and costumes, it always come down to the performance or performances of the live actors on the stage (or on the screen).

When actors hold their breath on stage, we in the audience also hold our breath. When actors heave breath in that soliloquy or climactic scene, we in the audience mimic (albeit internally) the heaving of that breath. It is that breath-use which takes us off guard, prepares us, and peels us out to that vulnerable place we have paid good money to be taken. And, if this doesn't happen, we leave the theater with a humble appreciation for the brilliant lighting, sets, and costumes.

•••

We are walking down the street; our breath is allowing us that function. We cross the intersection and barely miss being struck by a reckless driver. Our breath responds to the impulses, and our bodies move accordingly.

We are pretending to walk down the street; our breath is allowing us that function. We imagine crossing an intersection and visualize almost being struck by a reckless driver. If our bodies move accordingly our breath will respond to the impulses — and we will believe what we have concocted. And those observing this will also believe what is happening before their eyes. It has ceased (momentarily) to be the result of someone's potent imagination; it is real. Why? Because we (the observers) believe what the breath and body have told us. We want to believe. And when actors are un-believable, it is an extreme disappointment.

Movement, and the movement of the breath through the body, determine the level of believability in the actor's work. Since the voice is dependent on movement and breath, and the actor's emotional impulse is influenced by the mind *and* operated by the breath, it becomes obvious that the body and the breath do determine what is to appear and feel real to the observer. How often have you said to an actor: *You're holding your breath?* Pretty often, would be my guess. How often have you said to an actor: *You're using too much breath?* Not as often, although this, too, can be a problem, mostly due to a habitual breathing pattern when "performing" or "delivering lines."

What makes the breath issue a crucial and difficult one to address is the fact that, as humans, we respond to everything with breath. Some of the impulse responses **are** actually a holding of breath. That's just what we do, especially in moments of extreme fear, shame, guilt, and rage. So when we teach our actors *honest impulse*, which I do, we must also teach them how to finesse the natural impulses when those natural impulses do not serve the actor (or character).

I will ask Sarah to be in the moment of extreme fear for her life. She will work at that, and believe me, she will do her level best to live in that moment. Sarah instinctively will, at some point during her exercise, hold her breath because that is what humans do when confronted with sheer terror. The problem for Sarah is that she must speak most of the dialogue during the scene of sheer terror. Sarah needs to breathe freely in order to deliver her lines, to allow the audience to hear, and to function as an actress of worth. Sarah will need to modify her breathing, which instinctively is being told by her own "sense of reality in the moment" to hold her breath, thereby causing her to constrict her neck muscles, which will constrict her vocal mechanism. This is one of the conundrums of training actors: we work diligently to teach them some very difficult techniques or processes, which they must then turn around and contradict. Kind of like the English language: many rules; more exceptions to those rules.

•••

The internal process depends heavily on the actor's ability to access and utilize their own emotional machinery when portraying a character, and that begins with releasing control of the process, which is often aided by physical movement. Our actions, which quicken or slow our breathing, in turn can affect our emotions from moment to moment.

Actors need to know how to integrate a relaxed breathing state conducive to in-the-moment acting with the manipulation of breath to achieve a particular effect. For these functions to operate with seeming ease, the actor must understand the whole body or "mind/body" relationship and interplay between the body and breath. Yes, we know that neither exists without the other, but what we often forget is that *neither can create without the other.* We don't mean to forget, we're simply behaving humanly, we breathe involuntarily, so why would we be expected to constantly monitor our breath? The actor, on the other hand, must be trained to breathe in and out with minimal obstruction, and then be taught how to *physically* manipulate the breath, prior to learning how to use maximum breath for the desired outcomes.

•••

Only then will the actor's internal process take hold in a tangible way, and not remain an elusive "hit-or-miss" process.

4

SYNTHESIZING THE INTERNAL PROCESS: THE FINE LINE BETWEEN FOOL AND GENIUS

The internal process must not remain a hit-or-miss process; it must become a natural part of the actor's approach to every role. This is the goal. By the time the actor has created an internal process for himself, with your watchful guidance, he must be able to self-analyze without allowing the mind to take over the acting process (which results in the unobstructed flow of *honest impulse*). It is time for complex thought to enter the picture only when the actor knows how to act *in the moment*. And in order for complex thought to inform the actor fully, it needs to inform in a seemingly casual fashion. In other words, the actor must be in a place where "getting it right" is no longer a neurotic need. This means you need to allow the actor the space for making mistakes, wisely knowing that those "mistakes" will lead the actor to a better understanding of the task at hand. The popular way of saying this is that you need to allow the actor to *fail*. Personally, I've never been a fan of using the word failure when working with actors; they instinctively cringe at the word every time it is used when referring to their work. Yes, we all *understand* intellectually what it means, but the word sets off an unconscious alarm in the actor's head that needn't be present at all. *It wastes time.* That is why I am a big believer in using proper vocabulary in the studio, and ensuring that everyone involved in the studio adhere to the group's working vocabulary. I prefer that the actor learn that mistakes are merely a part of the process. Here is where actors who are willing to risk *being a fool* find it relatively easy to function. They understand that taking risks means risking looking like a fool. And that is perfectly fine with them.

•••

Roger has been working on his scene with Sarah. He and Sarah worked on the notes they received from their three actor-training instructors in the studio (movement, voice & speech, and acting.) They present the scene in class or the studio and Roger can't get past a small section of the scene, even though he's been "off book" (memorized) for some time now. He chastises himself for the mistakes because he and Sarah worked so hard and he let Sarah down and did not get to show how brilliantly they addressed the notes. And, to further complicate the situation, Sarah does not understand why Roger is so upset. She thinks he's being a bit self-centered, or, at best is acting like a big baby. What do you do? My suggestion – in this order – is that you: first, ignore Roger's impulsive over-reaction to his own work; second, praise them for obviously having addressed the notes from the three studio format professors; third, ask Sarah how the scene went before allowing Roger to speak. Most of the time, this will at least allow Roger to begin to redirect his focus, and you won't waste time on his neurotic ways.

•••

At this time, I think it important to explain a few things about proper procedure, or studio environment, as I see it. I don't talk about myself or my past "glories," unless it actually will help answer a question from one of the actors. Nothing bores actors, especially young actors, more than your going on and on about "the good ol' days when I was a such-and-such and I did that incredible thing." Don't get me wrong; they want to know about your experience, but you need to be wise about it, and allow them to get it out of you Actors love this. And this will not only endear them to you, this is an actual, very real part of the trust component. So, I don't allow them to get me to digress, until it is the right time. I allow them to think they have caused me to digress; this empowers them. Actors need to feel a certain amount of control, especially when you have scheduled the studio tightly. *Why* is this important? *Because it is one of the ways you tame the ego just long enough to train it.*

I rarely veer off what is scheduled for the day or week. Believe it or not, actors truly appreciate a somewhat rigid schedule. It will allow you to accomplish more with less time, and it will create time for impromptu discussions after second and final rounds of scene (or monologue) work. Leave time for discussion – they must get their questions answered, as much as possible. Nothing ticks off an actor more than not being able to speak his mind.

•••

So what exactly is the fine line between fool and genius? For me, it is that place where actors love to live. It is when the impulses are coursing through the body (acting and reacting) and the mind is allowing for the correct dialogue, well mannered and inflected. It is that place where actors feel as though they are flying. It is why most of us got into this business in the first place. When people speak of "getting bit by the acting bug," this is what they are talking about. I'm sure it is the same for dancers, singers, and musicians – any of the performing arts. When you are in this place, you honestly don't know if you came off as a fool to the audience or if your performance was sheer genius, because you were almost in an altered state. This sounds exciting, but not all novice actors experience this – not if their minds have never given up the driver's seat. And it's your job to instill in the actors *discipline* and to allow the actors *freedom*. One without the other is a waste of your and their time. Why? Because actors cannot learn discipline unless they have experienced true artistic freedom and they cannot experience true artistic freedom unless they have achieved well-balanced discipline. And, yes, this means that *you* must find both in your approach to training actors. You cannot discipline unless you have experienced true artistic expression, and you cannot express freely unless you have achieved well-balanced discipline in your work as a teacher, coach, or director.

This is why I do not believe in organic directing – the results are rarely wholly satisfying – something is always missing, and most of the time, it is difficult to put your finger on what it is. I do, however, believe in organic scene sessions within a well-structured rehearsal schedule. This ends up being about the actors and the script, and not about you. Most of the time, organic directing is more about the director and less about the actor and the script; it's more about how clever the director is, and less about the exquisite interplay between the characters. This is usually a young director's rite of passage. What I said about actors in Chapter One can be applied to young directors, coaches, and teachers: *Taking oneself too seriously is an obstacle that can be addressed; genuinely wanting to be sincere is not an obstacle at all.* And, as a reminder, I am lumping coaches, teachers, and directors together because all three end up functioning as one or all most of the time.

Acting and directing are both part of the same thing; they function as utilitarian tasks but one cannot exist without the other. This makes sense when we think about it, but we tend not to see what is right under our noses.

One of the best actor training exercises is to play one of Shakespeare's fools: Feste in *Twelfth Night*; Touchstone in *As You Like It*; The Fool in *King Lear*; Launcelot Gobbo in *The Merchant of Venice*; The Gravediggers in *Hamlet*; Launce in *Two Gentlemen of Verona*; Clown in *Othello, Measure For Measure*, and *The Winter's Tale*, and others. These "wise fools" encourage the actor to come to terms with his or her own silliness while speaking cleverly crafted, witty dialogue. This immediately demands intelligent choices and alacrity with language, both boisterous and subtle. Sounds, and most often song, also accompany the characters' modes of communication. All this, even at a glance, looks daunting, but for a true actor, it is the stuff that makes acting all the more worth the long hours of text analysis and physical/vocal rehearsal.

Who doesn't want to be a genius? Any of us would welcome the compliment. I'm talking about the non-measured compliment of "genius" level work: brilliance, as opposed to the IQ measurement. Modern and contemporary writers have picked up where Shakespeare left off; they have written characters that demand "silly brilliance" or "quirky honesty," or even "savant genius." Most mentally challenged characters in contemporary works of dramatic fiction are attributed with common sense. The true actor relishes all challenges, but particularly the challenges presented by these types of roles. These roles, whether they are Shakespearean or contemporary, present the actor with the opportunity to engage his body with cleverly crafted physicality. This, matched with witty or demanding language, is where an "actor's actor" dreams to live and re-live. It is absolute exhilaration to perform on the fine line between fool and genius. And this is the goal we must present our actors in order to encourage the internal process to synthesize organically.

Actors love to play fools and mentally or physically challenged characters but find it very hard to play *foolishly*, or even be a real fool. Why? Because many actors take themselves too seriously. Why do they take themselves so seriously? Where did they learn this? They learned it from us. If we take our art and ourselves too seriously, so will they. They will mirror us their mentors. *Taking oneself too seriously is an obstacle that can be addressed; genuinely wanting to be sincere is not an obstacle at all.*

Encourage your actors to play foolishly and risk being the fool, and engage them in a well-balanced manner: constructive criticism and praise; discipline and freedom. Your work with them will be absorbed and synthesized much sooner. Once an actor can perfect the fine line between fool and genius, they will more easily handle the stimulatingly dramatic and invigoratingly comedic roles.

•••

The actors will know themselves well enough to reveal comic bits of their humanity, whatever the genre.

PART II
EXTERNAL TECHNIQUE

5

COMEDY AND PING, PONG, AND PAUSE

Now that the training actor has a firm grasp of internal process, from an experiential standpoint, he or she is prepared for external technique, any technique or craft-oriented skill that demands a form of stylization in body, voice, and speech. Comedy, by its very nature, demands that the actor have a fundamentally sound relationship with timing and language. As you can see, already we are talking about "things external," so-called left-brained skills that can be more easily learned through practice. Yes, I do separate "things internal" from "things external." And I feel it's important that the actor in training also learn to at least visualize the difference. *Remember, our goal is to fine-tune the internal process, teach external technique, and teach the actor how to synthesize the two.* I've chosen to begin Part Two: External Technique with an examination of comedy, specifically classic comedy, because I feel it most clearly exemplifies what technique, an external event, is all about.

Robert Cohen, in his "career in acting" book, *Acting Professionally*, recognizes comedy and solo performance as, "…a great stepping stone to the stage or studio…" Stand-up comedians are the first to acknowledge how difficult comedy is. Most of us know comedy; we enjoy it, and we know what it is when we experience it. It doesn't take much to recognize it in others; it does, however, take much effort to develop it in ourselves. I recommend exploring the history of comedy via experiential exercise in addition to book-learning; most actor trainers would, too. The experiential training helps an actor fully grasp, internalize, and take ownership of the comedic work and the requisite stylization that accompanies it. And when we speak of history, the list of classic comedy works must include commedia dell' arte, the works of Jean Baptiste Poquelin Molière (in verse), and the works of Anton Chekhov. Yes, Chekhov. (More on that later in this chapter.)

COMMEDIA DELL' ARTE

From commedia dell' arte, the actor will learn that his or her core physicality, voice, speech, and gesture all work in synchronization to create lazzi, well-rehearsed comic bits of physical humor, oftentimes repeated. In movement training it is essential that neutral and commedia mask work accompany the study of commedia stock characters and scenarios. (Commedia masks represent a specific commedia stock character; neutral masks are purposefully vague, more avant-garde, and demand actor connection.) Voice training, including vocalization techniques that expand the range, should also accompany the study of commedia stock characters and scenarios that comprise the acting component of the training. This training in acting styles will allow the intermediate or advanced actor additional depth when engaging comic text and/or active impulse. And in time, it will inform the actor's approach to modern or contemporary material and roles.

Laban movement training is ideal for commedia styles work. It prepares the actor for flexible (in the literal sense) and detailed physical expression when embodying the commedia stock characters. Laban breaks down the flow, rhythm, purpose, and, if you will, psychology behind every move we make as humans and characters. Character movements for the zanni (clowns), the old men, the lovers, and other masked characters are all dictated by the mask, or in the case of the lovers, the make-up. Arlecchino's mask (Harlequin) demands a specific stance, walk, set of gestures, voice, and speech, while the Pantalone mask (an old, miserly, and lecherous man) calls for a different set of vocal expressions and physical stances or statements. Laban movement addresses these varied physical character statements with its extremely specific, anatomically accurate method of defining human movement.

The textbook that I require for the classic comedy styles semester is John Rudlin's *Commedia dell'Arte: An Actor's Handbook.*

Here is a sample entry from my college undergraduate BFA Acting syllabus:

COMMEDIA DELL' ARTE SCENE

Commedia dell' arte **stock characters** and brief scenarios will be explored. Each actor will then be assigned a scene and partner (or partners). Round one, round two notes and a final graded round. *Students are required to build and/or buy an inexpensive mask for their scene work. This unit of work is an exercise in adapting the actor's body to suit a particular character and character-style, using tools learned from movement oriented work in* **Laban,** *Alexander Technique, vocalization techniques and* **Formwork. A character** profile paper, based on the scene and textbook research, will be due on the day of first and second round presentations.** Thursday, February 25 – Tuesday, March 30. *Schedule will be distributed two weeks prior to first working day. 25% of course grade.*

MOLIÈRE

Once the intermediate acting student has begun to understand and master Laban movement terms, it is a perfect time for him or her to tackle the acting of characters who speak in verse language. Molière's language is an ideal bridge to Shakespeare for actors in training. The rhythmical comfort of Molière's rhyming couplets gives the actors-in-training confidence with something that might be foreign to them.

Why Molière in verse? Albeit in French, he wrote it in verse, and the *rhyming* verse is part of the comedy; that's what sets it apart, makes it special. Why some directors and producers do not believe that Molière in rhyming verse is "audience friendly," I cannot understand. (That rap and hip-hop implement rhyming language as a primary element should be evidence enough that humans love clever talk that rhymes, especially when it tells a story.) Why would anyone want to pay money to see Molière performed in prose? Richard Wilbur, translator of Molière (in verse), has made it easy for us; he's done all the work. All we need do is follow the rhythm and the music of the language, so to speak. The directors and producers who don't believe true Molière exists in *rhyming* verse are the same people who probably prefer Shakespeare in prose. (That's a joke.) I realize I'm in the minority here, but I am solid with this one. If you get it, and at least see my point, please let me know. I'd like to know your specific, personal reasons why *you* prefer Molière's rhyming verse.

When an actress-in-training can confidently deliver Molière in verse and take on the physical attributes demanded by the character, you (as the trainer) know she has come to terms with at least some of the intangibles of comedy. She has internalized the language to the point that humorous delivery of the verse is instinctive.

Here is a sample entry from my college undergraduate BFA Acting syllabus:

MOLIÈRE SCENE

A Molière play and characters will be assigned to scene partners. *The work will follow a process-oriented system created by your professors. This unit of work is designed to acquaint or re-acquaint you with the unique synthesis of Molière's language use, physical/vocal style and genre-acting style.* **A Character Profile paper will be due on the day of first and second round presentations.** Round One, Round Two notes and a final graded round. Thursday, January 17 – Tuesday, February 12. *Schedule will be distributed two weeks prior to first working day.* 15% of course grade.

•••

What's so funny? How often have you asked, or heard that question, especially when conversing with a good friend? We know what *that* is. We recognize it. That recognition is innately human. Yet, when the time comes to *be* funny, we sometimes clam up; not all of us, and maybe not you. But some actors find it difficult to *be* funny. Why? Usually it's because they are asked to think about the process of comedy, or the components of comedy, when all they need do is hang out with their good friends — then they're rightcback into what *that* is. So, why is comedy so difficult? Why does everyone keep telling us how difficult it is, as opposed to *"drama,"* which, many people say, isn't as difficult as comedy. Comedy, real comedy, isn't difficult at all — *when it happens* impulsively — in the moment. *In* the moment, in *that* moment, it appears to be, and feels effortless. It just happens. When this is the case, it appears to be effortless because it *is* effortless. So why does everyone keep saying comedy is hard? It isn't that comedy is hard; what's hard is the prep, everything that leads up to it: the environment, the scenario, the language, the situation, the chemistry, the rapport (or lack thereof), the body language, the style, the timing, and the humanity of it all, the *timing*...the moment. This is what aspiring actors struggle to understand and come to terms with...in this case, the moment of "funny." It could be a brush of the hand, the inflection and vocal pitch, the impressively rapid speaking, or any combination of factors. But it's funny. And the audience recognizes it because the actress knew exactly what she was doing; she knew how to get that laugh.

This is where I begin to separate myself from acting teachers who be-lieve that you cannot teach someone the skills of acting. Because I do. If it isn't clear up to now, I need to clarify that I believe anyone can be taught the skills, be given the tools, learn the craft of acting. How good they are with these tools separates the girls from the ladies and the men from the boys. Yes, of course, there's innate talent; we all recognize that. But we also recognize the difference between knowing something in our minds and knowing it in our whole being. Everyone can learn specific skills; most can affect those skills and display them in an adequate performance. Few can learn specific skills *and* seamlessly merge them to create a convincing per-sona.

Sometimes innate talent will not surface until a novice actor has mas-tered a few skills. Sometimes innate talent will not emerge until the novice actress has found the confidence to display a few skills that enable her to tap into something previously inaccessible. Because of instances such as these, I try my best to not give up on young actors, especially the ones who keep banging their heads against the wall in their efforts to "get it right," which, of course, they won't find until they release the *desire* to get it right. Ah, the *Zen* of Acting: it truly is difficult for young hearts to grasp.

CHEKHOV

Elizabeth Maupin, in the *Orlando Sentinel,* wrote the following regarding a production of Anton Chekhov's *The Sea Gull* at a local theater: "Actress Marty Stonerock likes to describe the plays of Anton Chekhov as if they were soap operas, or Seinfeld. Alan Bruun, artistic director of Mad Cow Theatre, compares them to *Survivor* (the TV reality show). Maybe that's an exaggeration. But finding ways to equate Chekhov with pop culture is an entryway for audiences – and theater people themselves – who are frightened to death of something Russian, something historical, something hard." Comparing Chekhov to *Survivor* is not that far-fetched when we put all Chekhovian and comedic factors in perspective.

Yes, most of Chekhov's work is comedic; he wrote comedies. He wrote a very specific type of comedy; it was satirical in nature and melodramatic in genre. And, I believe it's the melodramatic elements so prevalent in Chekhov's works that throws us off and makes it difficult to approach. Add to this the growing consensus that Chekhov was probably ahead of his time; he was writing during some very serious times, in the era of budding social revolutions in Russia. The logical conclusion is that Chekhov's "melodrama" is actually "drama." Why would most readers (and directors) stop to think otherwise? Russians are dead serious…and humorless. (That's a joke.) Of course, that's not true. So, to understand how to approach Chekhov, we need to have an educated and experiential (or kinesthetic) understanding of what satire is and what melodrama is. When is melodrama used in satire? In the USA, every Saturday evening on NBC-TV: on *Saturday Night Live.*

How does all this play into actor training? If an actor studies and acts Commedia and Moliere weeks before studying and acting Chekhov, it is very likely that the actor's approach to Chekhov (with your guidance) will retain a residue of stylistic satire, with a heavy dose of characterization, as they develop the dramatic (or melodramatic) elements in the Chekhovian scene they are presenting. That's the point in carefully bundling what your actors do in any given period of training.

Here is a sample entry from my college undergraduate BFA Acting syllabus:

CHEKHOV SCENE

A Chekhov play will be assigned to scene partners who will choose a scene from the play. *The work will follow a process-oriented system created by your professors. It is a three-round unit of work designed to hone acting style skills and synthesize your internal process and external acting-styles techniques.* **A Character Profile paper will be due on the day of first and second round presentations.** Round One, Round Two notes and a final round on the designated semester Final day. Thursday March 27 – Final. *Schedule with assigned play and partners will be distributed prior to first working day.* 25% of course grade.

Expect your actors to get frustrated as they struggle with the assigned Chekhov scenes; they want you to direct and tell them exactly what to do. They will want you to answer every single question they have regarding this odd blend of genre and style and motivation…and honest impulses. They will ask: "How can I be expected to play satire melodramatically, be serious about my character's intentions, *and* allow serious impulses to lead the way from moment to moment?" And, as I've previously stated, you must resist the temptation to direct them; if actors are not allowed to attempt and fail again and again, they will never make attempts that succeed when you are not around to direct them. Encourage them and be their devoted tour guide. Lift their spirits with exercises that will organically lead them to where you want them to go…which brings us to…

PING, PONG, AND PAUSE

So, what is this **Ping, Pong, and Pause**? In graduate school, many years ago, yet still very fresh in my memory, I was taught an exercise called "Ping, Pong, and Pause" by Jack Clay, my professional actor training professor, who had learned this simple exercise from Ms. Alvina Krause at Northwestern University. Over the years, I have found this exercise to be an essential tool for teaching actors how to *discover, sense,* and *feel* comic timing. And, mind you, this isn't something you experience once and you're done; quite the contrary. I implement this exercise when introducing a contemporary comedy unit and I use it again when teaching each of the classic comedy styles (Molière, commedia, and Chekhov); with this fun exercise, practice makes perfect and it spills over *immediately* into the scene or project at hand.

Ping, Pong, and Pause Exercise

Your scene pairings of two per scene will need a palm-sized bean bag (or palm-sized ball that has weight to it.) The bean bag is thrown back and forth **as** a line or phrase is spoken in the order it is spoken in the scene. The line begins as the actor is bouncing the bag in his or her hands and the line ends the moment the bag arrives in his or her partner's hands. A ping is a quick toss or zing of the bag to the partner (line is spoken rapidly). A pong is a lob, or slowly arched toss of the bag to the partner (line is spoken slowly). A pause is exactly that: a ...... *pause*, wherever needed.

Below is a brief example of how part of a Columbina and Capitano scene (exerpted from John Rudlin's *Commedia dell'Arte: an Actor's Handbook*) has been incorporated into a Ping, Pong and Pause exercise.

COLUMBINA: Slavering animal! *(pinged)*

CAPITANO: Beast of hell! *(ponged)*

COLUMBINA: Tinpot tyrant! *(ponged)*

CAPITANO: Monstrous manipulator! *(pinged)*

COLUMBINA: Look at this cur that's been beaten by every stick in the world! *(pause)*

CAPITANO: Pestilential appurtenance! *(pause)*

Timing is explored, lines are practiced with motivation, and peer pressure ensures that each round will be better than the last. Eventually the actors must use Ping, Pong, and Pause for the entire scene, after making character choices and memorizing lines. Soon after, the timing is internalized and feels perfectly natural.

•••

Making character choices is its own adventure.

6

THE ESSENCE OF CHARACTER

What is a character? It's a role in a play, screenplay, or teleplay. The word "character" has other meanings and usages. It's what we call someone who is "over-the-top" funny or "eccentric." It describes a person of integrity. There are character references and character sketches and if someone is "in character" they are keeping true to who they are portraying from beginning to end. If someone is "keeping in character," they are in harmony with who they are as a person; if someone is "out of character," they are out of harmony with their character's persona. When an actor "steps out of character," they have reverted to acting or reacting as themselves, the actor. When working with actors on characterization, it is important to keep all these definitions and usages in mind because they all come into play when constructing *characters.* Your "character" as the acting teacher, director, or coach will also play into how the actor processes the "building blocks," if you will, of *creating a role*, as Stanislavski put it.

Most actors in training come to you not knowing how to approach the process of creating characters; their model is, simply put, mimicry, which makes sense, as an initial attempt. Mimicking what a "character" does approximates a true portrayal, but this is a hit-or-miss way of creating characters because it is solely dependent on "other," something outside of our own experience. The best character actors in essence become the characters they are portraying; the only way you can become anything is to *be* it, to allow the characteristics to permeate you as a person. So, logic leads us to a process that allows actors to experience characteristics prior to "laying them on" or "taking them on" as a character, especially those with which they have no experience. And even if a novice, older actor has life experience to fall back on, it is still a struggle to take on the experiences and outlook of another.

The **first** task is to allow the training actor to "live with," however temporarily, a character's physicality, vocal patterns, speech sounds, and personality traits. The **second** task is to take the actor to a place of honest impulse *while* portraying the character so the actor begins to feel as though the character he is portraying is a "second skin." Character template monologues are the best way to practice synthesizing the steps that a gifted actor instinctively takes when creating a role. But remember, some actors in training are not instinctual, thus the need to take them step-by-step until they begin to experience the character from moment to moment.

CHARACTER TEMPLATE MONOLOGUES – (*the **first** task*)

One of my colleagues, Jennifer Mizenko, a gifted Movement for the Actor professor, I might add, coined the term "template" to describe a one-minute monologue that is to be used for several assignments throughout an extended period of time. The template is a handy monologue for the student actor to use throughout the semester or month-long workshop. This is a true time saver for everyone, especially the student or studio actor. It can also assist the actor to synthesize the training if the same template monologue is used for work in acting class, movement class, and voice and speech class during a semester or workshop.

The **Character Template Monologue** utilizes the same process to explore both the comedic and dramatic aspects of a role. For the actor to draw maximum benefit from this work, allow enough time to explore, present, and perform both characters (comedic and dramatic). You can choose to use the same "template" monologue for both (comedic and dramatic) or you can have the actor choose a one-minute monologue for comedic and a different monologue for dramatic.

1.   Soliciting suggestions from the group, list on a chalkboard ten signature personal characteristics in each category:

Voice	Speech	Physical	Personality Traits
1	1	1	1
2	2	2	2
3	3	3	3 .....

2.   Pair up (actor; character partner).

3.   Character partner will choose one characteristic from each of the four lists and the actor will explore one at a time (give actors at least two minutes to explore each characteristic). Tell them the moment before they begin a new one, but don't tell them all four before you begin with the first.

4.   Actors use the four characteristics to create a character that speaks for two minutes. (Character partners need to keep their actors focused on the four characteristics, much like a "director.")

5.   Each actor presents his or her character to the class, using improvisation phrases and words that impulsively surfaced during the exploration.

6.   Actors switch places with their character partners and go through steps 3 through 5 again.

Again, the **exploration** portion of this work is the same for both the comedic and dramatic portrayals. Once you have gone through the weeks of work exploring a comedic character, go through the same exploration portion of the work when beginning the process of exploring a dramatic character. Note that the actors need to be encouraged to go as far as possible with all their choices: vocal, speech, physicality, and personality trait; if not encouraged to risk failure, they will tend to hold on to their fears of the unknown and not truly *explore* new territory.

For those of us who are coaching, teaching, or directing actors, we often forget how fragile training or novice actors are; they are being asked to produce on a consistent basis and one of the major obstacles actors face is the consistent blow to the ego that the acting (or entertainment) profession doles out. So, yes, it's good that they learn how to "toughen up," so to speak, in order to best succeed in the business. *But,* our job isn't only to prepare them for the worst; *our* job is to prepare them to succeed at *their* best. And in order to get there they must learn how to stay positive about their work and the characters (all unique) that only *they* can create. If you dwell too much on how tough the business is, you will *never* allow that "diamond in the rough" to learn from *you* and go on to be a great artist or entertainer. This attitude, approach, or character trait in you will create a bond of trust that you cannot buy, borrow, steal, or fake your way through.

CHARACTERS AND SCENEWORK – (*the **second** task*)

When your actors have secured a personal process by which to approach characters, at least an initial one, they are ready to put this procedure to the test with 20th century realism characters, which they must acquaint themselves with prior to tackling 20th century stylistic characters, such as those in the works of Harold Pinter (stylized drama), Georges Feydeau (classic farce), Samuel Beckett (absurdism), and Tom Stoppard (stylized dramatic comedy). Twentieth century realism characters will require just enough style that the actor is allowed to remain close to his or her own experience, thus avoiding possible rejection or fear of "period demands." Again, the unknown is always the major obstacle. During this realism work, in the assigned scene, you will address *the **second** task* – merging a "second skin" character with honest impulse. "Merging" is a word I choose purposefully. Again, it isn't *what* we need do next that is important; what's important is ***how*** we do it. Positive results are deeply embedded in the ***how***. The most exciting part of this for the actor is working opposite a scene partner. They are aware that the true test of any acting work is when the actor is creating action with another actor in a scene, giving and taking when speaking and listening.

This is when you must demand **honest impulses** from the actors **as** they attempt to craft a character. The characterizations might seem "external," or put-on, so to speak; this is understandable — you're working on external technique. But *your* job is to keep each moment honest, connected to their personal experience, and embedded in some reality of their own. As long as you keep your goal, or goals, in mind, you will not fail. As long as you remain true to each moment they create in their scene, and, in turn, demand honest impulses from them as they work, you will not fail. They can fail, and stumble, and regroup, because that is the process, but you will not have failed yourself or them, your actorsr

While the acting component of the training focuses on the Realism scene-network, it is the perfect time for the voice/speech component of the work to engage the actors in Shaw monologues, (monologues from the works of George Bernard Shaw). Shaw's language is demanding, yet, for the most part, realistic; Shaw's characters often demand idiosyncratic behavior that mirrors the language, thus making it an enticing bridge toward characterization. Shaw's language almost demands "character" in the actor's physicality and timing choices when performing action and instinctual reaction. The Shaw monologues (paired with Skinner targeting [speech] assignments, which I will detail in the next chapter) will enhance the actors' confidence and provide a safe haven, a solace to reference when attempting any and all "characters."

After feeling confident with realism characters, now that the actor understands and trusts his or her choices when creating a "character," it is time for them to tackle the genres that demand distinct styles, such as those of the aforementioned playwrights: Pinter, Feydeau, Beckett, and Stoppard.

We might want to consider this a *third task*, or step, but, by this time, you and your actors are simply applying external technique based on the demands of genre, each distinct, each pleading for a sense of its own style from you and the actor. Pinter's works will demand an understanding of silence, pauses, timing, and action that often isn't paired with dialogue. Feydeau's works will demand fleeting language and physicality that must be paired with exact, razor-sharp timing when speaking *and* moving. Beckett's works will demand an "existential" relationship with time and comedy, meaning absolute honest impulses when taking action and speaking *and* "living in silence." Stoppard's clever language spirals will demand a specific understanding of meaning from one moment to the next, which will facilitate learning how to build intensity in a monologue and in scene units. Hopefully, the actors are learning well from their Shaw monologue work in the voice and speech component of the training.

Everything I have so far detailed in this chapter is a healthy description (in a nutshell) of what is taught in the sophomore acting studio on the college level of actor training. In the BFA acting studio, comprised, for the most part, of juniors and seniors in college, with an occasional non-traditional (middle-aged) student actor, the essence of external technique and the practice of characterization resides in the *layering* of voice work, physicality/movement work, speech/dialect directives, and work with the psychology of the characters, including psychological gesture, when addressing any playwright's work.

•••

When you get down to it, voice, speech, and movement are the foundation, the essence of actor training.

7

LANGUAGE, TEXT, AND TIMING
(VOICE, SPEECH, AND PHYSICALITY)

Unless a character remains silent throughout the course of an entire production, actors primarily use voice to communicate purpose, motivation, and tactics. A serious actor needs a well-trained voice. What if an actor isn't serious about his or her voice? That's fine, but they must know that they are taking their chances and so are you, if you don't explain this. At the callback or screen test, the actor's voice seals the deal, so to speak; her appearance might break the ice, but the voice is the deal breaker.

I began the teaching side of my career as a young voice and speech teacher. After studying briefly with Kristin Linklater, (the author of *Freeing the Natural Voice*) on the heels of having studied intensely with Margaret Loft for many years at Southern Methodist University, I found myself, in a matter of mere months, training graduate and undergraduate students voice and speech at the University of Michigan. Having been first solely a voice and speech teacher gave me the foundation for teaching acting. That is when I began to fully comprehend that we as actor trainers need a comprehensive knowledge of the actor's instrument(s) in order to successfully train actors; without this kinesthetic understanding, we might find ourselves guessing a bit too much. And nothing irritates actors more than playing guessing games with the people who have been "authorized" to train them.

VOICE

Voice is an event requiring muscle, breath, thought, and impulse. The main thing you need to know about voice is that your actors need to breathe freely, openly, and honestly when performing. The moment you observe them holding their breath or tightening their core, neck, or joints, you can be sure that the voice they are using is not connected to honest impulse. The resulting performance will seem, and sound, fake. This is a bit simplistic, but so much of vocal training goes back to breath. And much of the breath work is dependent on a flexible and freely moving body; in short, a body that benefits from movement training. Daily ribcage/breath expansion exercises are recommended for the actor's vocal improvement; and at least twice weekly the actor needs to physically work with the muscles and membranes that increase resonance in the head (upper range), mouth (mid-range), and chest (lower range).

As an acting teacher, coach, or director of actors, you understand enough of how it all works; you needn't be an expert voice instructor (or movement specialist) to be an expert with actors. Of course, any knowledge of the specializations helps: voice, speech, movement, stage combat, mask work, etc. Your additional specialization, *your* knowledge, helps you to be a better acting teacher, coach or director of actors. And whatever your additional specialization voice work is important. If you are familiar with vocal performance (singing), your in-depth knowledge has served you well. You've probably noticed the difference in the actors' voices when singing and when speaking. Some (even exquisite) singers do not translate the basics to speaking, when they are acting in a scene; some do. The point is that **voice for the actor** is a discipline unique to speaking, as opposed to vocal performance (singing.) This is the number one thing you must come to terms with. Come to understand the similarities and the differences.

Many young (or novice) actors come to you having been in some type of choir or with some kind of singing background, however basic. *Most* young (or novice) actors come to you with minimal or no understanding of what voice for the actor means. In fact, the most frequently asked question I get when it comes to anything related to voice for the actor is: "What's the difference between voice and speech?" That's a good question; it means the actor is already beginning to understand that there must be a difference since the two are separated by an "and." My answer is always the same:s"Voice is the release of sound; Speech is the articulation (or shaping) of that sound." Notice I avoided the word "production," as in "voice pro-duction."

There is nothing wrong with the term "voice production," as long as the people using and hearing the term know the actual organic or "natural" process that takes place when speaking is connected to impulse and breath. The problem I have with the term (and I'm not the only one) is that less ex-perienced actors take the word "production" and translate it into something "forced," something "overly-manipulated." Yes, there are muscles at work when we are performing and speaking on stage or speaking in the sound stage or speaking on location. But the moment the actor in training thinks he is supposed to force, thus straining his voice, all hopes for natural sound and honest impulse go out the window, because he is preoccupied with forc-ing something that depends on free-flowing breath and impulse, not just muscle and thought. Most, if not all, voice for the actor trainers would agree with this statement.

These are some of the bits of information that result from experience and daily exposure to the challenges that come with training actors. If you require further study, the most influential voice and speech "gurus" are: Kristin Linklater, Cicely Berry, Arthur Lessac, Patsy Rodenburg, Catherine Fitzmaurice, Mary Corrigan, Bonnie Raphael, and Dudley Knight. The best, and most current, information regarding voice and speech training can be found on the website of the Voice and Speech Trainers Association (VASTA). http://www.vasta.org/.

MOVEMENT

Before moving on to my comments and information regarding speech, in order to remain as "organic" as possible, I must next address movement, movement training, and how methods and disciplines can alter the vocal product in positive and negative ways. You'll notice that my very first describer for "voice" was "muscular." That's right. You cannot train an actor's voice unless you also train the actor's body. All the breath work, thought, and impulse work will almost be a waste of time, unless the actor's musculature is attended to. Does this mean that every actor has to have a perfect physique? No, no. In fact, too much muscle in the wrong places can actually prevent the breath from moving and functioning properly. So, does this mean all actors have to have flabby bellies in order to speak magnificently? No. The muscles need to be toned properly, and any type of physical activity will do the trick. If your high school or college or professional studio does not have access to a theatre movement professional or specialist, any type of physical activity that involves frequent and active breathing will work: yes, send your actors out the door for a quick jog at the top or middle of every session. But, if you want better results, you might want to find the movement discipline or disciplines that will best fit or match the focus of your program and the varied methods your staff utilizes. The most popular are the movement works of these practitioners and trailblazers: Feldenkreis, Bogart, Roth, Suzuki, Pisk, Humphries, Barba, and Grotowski. But Jacques Lecoq's spatial physical techniques, F. Matthias Alexander's technique of lengthening, re-alignment, and releasing, and Rudolph Laban's movement philosophy and system(s), in my opinion, are the best for actors, especially if money, time, or personnel are issues.

The Alexander Technique is a perfect introduction to movement work. It has benefited actors, athletes, dancers and musicians by reeducating the body to move more efficiently and get rid of accumulated patterns of tension. It improves overall ease of movement and coordination and helps to undo habits of harmful obstructive movements. It will also allow the actor to practice internally focused concentration, a skill that changes with time and aging, a skill that actors need to keep in mind long into their careers. (I will provide more detailed information regarding the Alexander Technique in upcoming chapters.)

The work of Jacques Lecoq trains actors through highly physical work with buffoonery, clowning, games that explore actors' physical orientation with objects and studio space, and commedia dell'arte. This work is highly stylized and demanding. Some of the practices and exercises are fun and engaging, and you will find them very helpful, but to become an expert in Lecoq it takes years of training and meticulous athletic skill.

In 1948, Rudolph Laban created the Art of Movement Studio in Manchester, England. His work centered on the art of dance, but as the decades have rolled by, more and more actor trainers have come to depend on his system and notation to document and translate movement. Although the notation was primarily created to document works of dance choreography, its "language" of symbols has come to describe the general movement of the human being. The study of BESS (body, effort, shape, and space) provides the actor with a movement vocabulary that translates into physical statements, which, in turn, draw a corresponding "e-motion-al" expression from the actor. As I mentioned earlier, I have learned much from working with my colleague, Professor Jennifer Mizenko, who is an expert movement for the actor trainer. What is so exciting to me is watching the Laban work, as it progresses, mirroring the acting work in the studio, and permeating the actors' imaginations and physical/vocal expressions. Then, it is ultimately satisfying to see this physical knowledge translate into choices of character portrayal and scene structure, especially when the studio is studying acting styles in classic comedy or classic drama. I have found the Laban work to be perfect for actor training purposes.

So what could possibly be "negative" about any type of movement training? Curiously, I have found ballet to create detrimental physical restrictions for the actor. Ballet is based on the "positions" and the basis of the "positions" is the "turnout" from the hip sockets. This forced "deforming" of the natural structure of the body (at its core) creates vocal problems for some actors – not all. (At this point, I must share that I personally love ballet, and revere those who can create balletic magic on the stage and who devote their beings to this art.) Ballet does not help the actor find a truly open, freely-flowing, resonant voice. It pains me to state this; nonetheless this has been my experience throughout decades of training actors.

SPEECH

Speech, the teaching of articulating text, is the most challenging of the actor-training disciplines because it takes a great ear to teach speech and a determined actor, with an equally great ear, to absorb and practice, practice, practice. When learning how to correct regionalisms (regional dialect reduction), an actor must carefully listen and learn to reduce deviations from the desired accent. This is the actor's first step towards eliminating bad habits that prevent the voice from serving as a strong conduit of emotional expression. Then, on top of that, they may need to learn to speak different dialects! How's that for a speech journey?

The International Phonetic Alphabet is the primary tool used by most who teach or coach corrective speech, regionalism reduction, Standard American, RP (Received Pronunciation), and a globe full of dialects. Every actor needs to, at the very least, have a basic knowledge of these symbols and their accompanying sounds. IPA is broken down into individual phonemes (symbols), which are used to symbolize vowel, consonant, diphthong (pronounced **dif**-thawng), and cluster combinations. Written with phonemes, the word "diphthong" looks like this: [dɪfθɔŋ]. Notice that the "**ph**" is one sound, the "**th**" is one sound, and the "**ng**" is one sound. Each of these sounds has its own symbol, and this ingenious international alphabet can represent sounds in all languages. Therefore, it is a practical notation for actors to learn, especially if the actor intends to learn how to speak in various dialects or accents. And, of course, the more dialects an actor has access to, the more acting work he or she will land, especially when starting out.

American Theater Standard Speech has many names: Mid-Atlantic, Eastern Standard, Stage Standard, Skinner Standard, American Stage Speech; and I am sure the list goes on. Whatever it's called, it was established by Edith Skinner, in her book, *Speak With Distinction*, and when she taught at the Julliard School, Yale School of Drama, the Tisch School at NYU, and American Conservatory Theatre. Along with teaching this "standard" manner of speech for the stage, Ms. Skinner taught what she called targeting, a method of "scoring" your script (or text) with symbols that created or enhanced inflection, rhythm, build, tempo, and emphasis. I have found that the works of George Bernard Shaw are perfect for targeting. The "heightened language" of G.B. Shaw forces actors to speak with the use of inflection, rhythm, build, tempo, and emphasis very well-suited for targeting analysis. Most of his monologues cannot be spoken without a natural build to a big finish. In addition, Shaw's language is the perfect bridge to Shakespeare, especially for actors who fear attempting, much less speaking, Shakespearean language.

SCANSION WITH SHAKESPEARE

After your actors have learned how to target G.B. Shaw's language and perform or present it aloud, they should be ready to tackle the scansion of William Shakespeare's blank verse.

To take the fear out of acting Shakespeare, the actor must first learn scansion and know what he or she is saying when speaking. The best resource I have found is Joseph Olivieri's *Shakespeare Without Fear*. This exceptional book details the use of blank verse, rhyming verse, compression, expansion, the use of iambic pentameter, and the, at times, differing aspects of the written and spoken Shakespearean word. (Shakespeare's works were meant to be spoken/performed and not merely read; the speaking of Shakespeare's heightened language is a learned skill.) Should you be searching for a detailed step-by-step manual regarding scansion, this may be what you're looking for. The research and scholarship that went into writing Olivieri's incredible resource is commendable. After reading this book, you will understand why many actors further their studies at a graduate acting school. Scansion isn't easy and it isn't something you can learn in a matter of months.

Actors must understand what they are saying. Prior to working with scansion on paper, they should do their dictionary and pronunciation homework, which is basic work for all actors, young and old, novice or professional. As a part of the first attempts to speak the scansion-notated text, I find it helpful to have the actors literally sing their text as if it were an opera or operetta. In fact, "ballet operinas" is what I have labeled this step; I have students pretend they are singing opera as they move in a balletic fashion. It breaks the ice, and in a lighthearted way it allows the actor to truly explore what scansion is all about – rhythm, meter, flow, build, and enunciating the meaning of the word through sounds and movements. It was G.B. Shaw who said about Shakespeare's language: "The chant is endless." Soon the actors will internalize the meaning with the meter and find their distinct way of communicating the character's thoughts and actions, in essence placing their personal mark on the "interpretation" of the character.

•••

Successful actors know the intrinsic importance of voice, speech, and physicality in communicating intent and emotion; more importantly they are able to link the physical processes of movement and speech with language, text, and timing. Yes, some super humans are born with this "connective" gift. Some of them love language and sound so much they find it easy to "characterize." These lucky folks have substantial careers as voice actors; they provide voices for animation or voice-overs for commercials, television/film, dubbings, and network animation hits. One of my former "classically trained" students, Bill Fagerbakke is the voice of Patrick Star in the television animation hit, *SpongeBob SquarePants*, among other well-known television and film roles.

•••

Understanding text and converting it to the spoken word, complete with natural cadence, timing, and inflection is a talent, but it can certainly be learned with much practice, practice, practice.

8

THE ETERNAL, HONEST IMPULSE AND DRAMATIC TECHNIQUE

Most "Best Performance by an Actor (or Actress) in a Leading Role" recognitions are awarded to actors who perform something dramatic in nature. But if comedy is supposedly more difficult in general, then why not, at least occasionally, award comedic performances? Is it because we respect dramatic performances more than comedic? I don't think so. Is it because we love the catharsis of a moving and serious, or tragic, subject matter? Maybe. The Greeks thought so. Is it because we take ourselves too seriously? Probably. Is it because the actor happened to perform serious matter in a film or stage production that was relevant to the times? Likely. Or is it that the actor did something "brave" by revealing to the world a part of herself that we find very difficult to share, much less talk about? Yes. Acting awards are presented to actors who do something special, something we secretly fear; that's why it's considered brave. You ask every single actor who has won a Best Performance Award and they will tell you that they were just doing their job, that it wasn't a "courageous act" to perform the role. They were most happy, elated, in fact, to perform the role. That's what they live for. Why? Because most actors need to mirror the world they live in. They live to take on a new challenge right around the corner, after this one is done. They love to test just how human they really are, because it is their personal connection to their humanness that they treasure. And so do you.

Many actors openly discuss the "high" they get from performing dramatic roles. Some talk about their "addiction" to this high. I don't know if it's adrenaline; I'm not a medical professional. What I do know is that many actors, especially young actors, find themselves attracted to the art of acting due primarily to this feeling of completion in their beings. There are some actors, especially young actors, who are attracted to this feeling for the wrong reasons, if there's such a thing. What are the wrong reasons? Acting is not, and should not be viewed as, therapy. Actors joke about certain roles having been "therapeutic" at the time they performed them; most are doing just that, joking. Some are not joking and they find themselves in a "rabbit hole" that has more to do with their problems than the art form. For these young actors, I always recommend that they settle the issues then come back to the training, because, despite the cleansing benefits they might occasionally experience from these roles, acting is not therapy. (Role playing has been found to be extremely successful by some professional therapists, especially in drama therapy.) But the craft itself must always be viewed through an artistic lens, so to speak. It is the only way the actor will learn the craft as separate from his or her personal life. Having said that, there is a bit of a contradiction here; it is the actor's personal experience that he must draw from in order to successfully perform most dramatic roles. So, what's an actor to do? I urge actors to remain professional, to leave the work at the workplace. This is easier said than done, for most of us. But it's the only way an actor will find fulfillment in work and life.

DRAMATIC TECHNIQUE

In Chapter Two, I described **honest impulse** as an "organic event that occurs in the immediate moment characterized by a wholly integrated, singular, and clear action." The operative word is *"clear."* It is the clarity of thought and action that give the impulse its *honest* attributes, no matter how impulsive it may seem. Some improvisation, though seeming impulsive, might not be very "honest." What is calculated? What's a real risk? What's a calculated risk? You get my meaning.

An actor draws from his personal experience and shares these impulses through the veil of the character in order to communicate something important in that singular moment in time. This is the crux of the theatrical experience, the essence of theatre. Throughout human history, from tribal ritual to Greek tragedy on through Shakespearean drama to the cop and doctor dramas on contemporary television, the qualifier of the work's aesthetics has always been the impact of the pivotal moments in the drama. Are we moved? And by how much? It is the *quality* of the drama that defines the particular human condition scrutinized in the dramatic work. It's the honest impulses that elevate good drama to the sublime, because when the portrayal is real, we, the audience, come along on the emotional journey.

Earlier in this book, I also described the internal process, which is the foundation of dramatic technique. Because the internal process is so personal in nature and so unique to each actor, it is difficult to evaluate progress, yet relatively simple to evaluate the final product. How often have you heard, "You know it when you see it on the stage" regarding an actor's performance? That's what the audience pays money to see, but the actors need a system, a process in order to *get there*; that's our job as trainers, to help them get there. I use the works of dramatic playwrights to help me set landmarks, or goals, for the actors to work toward and accomplish. (Remember, the actor must always feel some kind of forward *progress*, since progress is so slow at times and can be elusive.) Using the playwright's works, I set out to teach each playwright's unique style of communication; in most cases the stylistic idiosyncrasies are a significant contributor to a genre. So we set out to create specific "styles" pertaining to each playwright's work, beginning with Henrik Ibsen.

Ibsen's naturalism, commentaries on 19th century social structures and mores, lend themselves to emotional conflicts ideal for training actors. In addition, the 19th century manner and dress demand characterization from the actor as (s)he delves into the scene to recreate angst and agitation. By now your actors should know how to combine specific physical stylistic movement with movement generated by an honest human urgency based on how they themselves would respond to a challenge. (If an actor playing

Nora or Hedda says, "but I can't move that way when I'm angry," they don't belong in this advanced studio. Nonetheless, your answer must be: "*You might not move that way, but Nora would, in her world, given her circumstances.*")

In your acting studio program, I cannot stress enough how important it is to coordinate the speech, movement, and acting components. For example, as the actors work on Ibsen scenes, the speech professor or instructor should use one of the Ibsen monologues (from their acting scene) to work with in speech class; likewise, the movement professor or specialist must work on period dance and/or period movement in the semester or year that the actors are learning dramatic styles. That's the only way to achieve a true *synthesis*; it's the best way to ensure that your students will become successful working actors, highly sought-after artists, or valuable professionals in the arts, theatre, or entertainment industry. Remember, many actors in training do not end up in the acting profession but that doesn't mean they can't be as successful contributors, whatever the field. What they learn in actor training is going to make them a more successful, better-adjusted person. Coordinate components and make built-in synthesis a hallmark of your acting program.

Shakespearean monologues need to be practiced before tackling Shakespearean scenes. The actors need to apply scansion, decode language, and work on pronunciation prior to tackling a scene; it will give them the space to concentrate on their work prior to collaborating with a scene partner. It's important the actors work with *blank verse* monologues (and scenes) since the goal is to explore scansion, targeting, and becoming familiar with the ten syllable lines of verse. (Blank verse is unrhymed language written in iambic pentameter.) The following list of steps is what I use; keep in mind that the ultimate goal is for the actors to speak the language as if it were their own. The steps are a technical process.

SEQUENCE OF INSTRUCTIONAL STEPS FOR
SHAKESPEAREAN MONOLOGUE

ROUND ONE: (Each actor works individually)

1. SCANSION AND TARGETING

2. PRONUNCIATION AND MEANING

3. BREAK/CATCH-BREATH AT END OF EVERY
    10 SYLLABLE LINE

4. FULL STOP AT PERIODS AND COLONS

5. SPEAK THE MEANING: Catch breaths and full breaths only
    to support meaning without breaking the rhythm of the meter

6. VERSE & MOVEMENT: Releasing meaning and language via
    the body (similar to a simple sound and movement exercise, but
    with verse language)

In the second round presentations of their monologues they are provided written notes from all three instructors: acting, voice/speech, and
movement, prior to their third, and final, round performance.

•••

After the monologue work the actors should explore Shakespearean
scenes; the actors should be encouraged, if not expected, to work on their
own scansion, targeting, pronunciation, meaning, and verse work, prior to
their first round presentation of their scene (on book andwith scripts in
hand).

SEQUENCE OF INSTRUCTIONAL STEPS FOR SHAKESPEAREAN SCENEWORK

EXPLORATION DAY:

1. Each scene explores scansion/prose language, pronunciation and meaning
2. Each scene explores breaking at the end of every 10 syllable line
3. Each scene explores full stops at periods and colons
4. Each scene explores what it is to SPEAK THE MEANING: Catch breaths and full breaths only to support Meaning without breaking the rhythm of the meter

ROUND ONE: (Each actor works individually, then with partner)

1. ACT THE MEANING: Catch breaths and full breaths only - to support meaning without breaking the rhythm of the meter

2. **WORDZZ** & MOVEMENT: Releasing meaning and language out the body – with the help of two volunteers (*the next scene to go up*), feeding the words to actors as they work. (I pruposely use "z"s to stress sound use.)

3. AFFECT YOUR PARTNER: with Wordzz and movement and imagery – send sounds through your body to your partner, make note of rhythms/patterns

4. SUBTEXT WITH PARTNER: Volunteers – inner monologue/ dialogue – images – with the help of two volunteers (*the next scene to go up*), feed images/impulse responses to actors as they work through the scene.

ROUND TWO:

Evaluated on paper by profs (and notes from class) on the following:
Scansion
Emotional commitment
Character development
Voice
Character movement
Character profile paper
Progress on challenges and/or acting problems
Language use: communication of text, speech, meaning, pronunciation
Synthesis of internal process and external technique
Progress on achieving character profile goals

ROUND THREE: (Final round - all actors perform on the same day)

All evaluated on round two assessment categories

•••

I have found it useful, between the Shakespearean monologue unit and scenework, to have the actors in the studio work on a quickly scheduled comedic scene by Oscar Wilde or Noel Coward. These two playwrights were greatly influenced by Shakespeare's writing and the stylistic banter of the language and whimsical physicality of the period characters are a welcomed and seemingly easy break from Shakespeare's drama. I say *seemingly* for a reason: the actors will settle into the Wilde and Coward styles like ducks to water, having been bombarded by all the work on Shakespeare's language. Had I scheduled the Wilde/Coward scenes prior to any Shakespearean work, the baggage of doubts would have been an added obstacle; this strategy is seemingly simple, but pedagogically valuable.

•••

Again – it isn't so much what you do; it's *how* you do it that matters.

9

"CREATING AGAIN" IN THE MOMENT

How is it possible to remain "in the moment" with every performance of the same role, night after night, or the same role in the same scene, take after take? The best professional actors deliver with every performance and camera take by staying focused on the reality of the character's given circumstances; in the business it's called "staying in the moment." How does an actor do that? How do we train actors to do that?

Most actors, when asked how they deliver the same great performance night after night or camera take after camera take, will tell you they stay focused on recreating what they've done before That's logical, and this would be correct for professional, well-seasoned actors who have a process for making this happen. For young (or novice) actors, on the other hand, especially actors in training, the word "recreate" can be a trap. That is why I differentiate between "recreating" and "creating again." Too often, even seasoned actors fall into the trap of attempting to recreate a particular performance or end product. (In the Alexander technique, there is a term called "end-gaining," which is an attempt to reproduce the end result without going through the mind/body primary orders, which get the body to a neutral, aligned place.) Hilary King defines **end-gaining** as "the tendency we have to keep our mind and actions focused on an end result whilst losing sight of, and frequently at the expense of, the means-whereby." "Recreating" is somewhat similar to "end-gaining" in that the attempt to recreate what's been done before places more emphasis on the end product rather than the character's environment and the physiological realities of the actor during a particular day or moment. We humans change from day to day, often from moment to moment; we aren't in the same mental and emotional place today as we were yesterday; our mental, physical, and emotional landscapes change. Human beings, especially artists, are mercurial..

I encourage actors to create the **environment**, the **physiological state**, and **scenario-based motivations** every time they approach the character's world; I ask them to "create again," so it is always a fresh, new performance for the audience, because the audience is experiencing that performance for the first time. Actors depend on us coaches, directors, and trainers to remind them; they expect these reminders; they need them. Remember that they, the actors, are deep inside the world of the play or scene, or should be. We are outside, looking in and are expected to remain as objective as possible; they, the actors, expect absolute objectivity from us.

So how does an actor know when he or she is "in the moment?" The manifestations of acting "in the now" are numerous and intangible, but I will attempt to describe them. I know most of you have run across this: the actors think they just performed their best show, while most in the audience would disagree; or the audience loves the production and the work, giving it a standing ovation, while the actors are dumbfounded because they are all in agreement that their work that night frankly stunk. These incongruous perceptions are some of the intangibles. But again, even these contrasting perceptions are just that, perceptions, and I believe they fall into the "recreating" trap because they are mostly related to the end product. Actors know they are "in the moment" when they are exhausted from having relived the character's **journey**, and, most of the time, are not cognizant of the passage of **time** on stage or in front of the camera. Staying connected to the world of the play or environment throughout the performance or shoot demands **staunch concentration**, and uninterrupted concentration and concurrent mental fatigue are indicators that the actors succeeded in remaining "in the moment."

Good actors tend to be extremely observant individuals; they can scan whatever environment they find themselves in and adapt. They can also fabricate an environment for their character and keep it real for the duration of the performance or shoot. But even the best actors can be distracted by an audience member or by a member of the film crew. Theatre lore abounds regarding just these instances; granted, it is easier to recover from the distraction when performing a comedic role; in these comedic instances, the best actors find a way to incorporate the distraction into the action or motivation at hand. For novice actors, distraction tends to be one of the major obstacles to learning how to remain "in the moment." The same gift for scanning an environment and adapting can become a novice actor's Achilles' heel. Exercises that develop sharp focus and concentration, or years of acting experience, seem to be the only methods to combat a tendency toward easy distraction. Some young (or novice) actors never get past these moments of distraction when performing; these would-be actors need to address their focus-related obstacles prior to returning to the training. Either way, they've learned a valuable bit of information; the lack of concentration or focus is a problem when acting a role. Keen focus and alert concentration are the keys to success, whatever the field.

•••

When I recognize that an actor is "recreating" a role in the studio, I pause and tell them, "You're attempting to recreate what you did yesterday. You need to create everything fresh for today, for the present, instead of attempting to recreate yesterday's really good work." "I really don't know what you mean, Joe. I understand it in my head, but I don't know what to do with it," is a common answer, until they get it, after much practice. And I reply, "Well, let's go through each step; that's why you're here."

"Place yourself and your character in the environment; tell me where you are." They do so. "Now place yourself in the moment before this scene; tell me what's happening." They do so. "Now let's re-enact that moment before – just you and your scene partner." They do so. "Now continue with the scene after approximately two minutes' worth of your moment before, but you must promise to stop the moment you lose your connection to each action or moment." They do so, and stop when their focus wanes. "Why did you stop?" They answer, "I stopped feeling it." I reply, "So? I thought you stopped because you lost your connection to the action or moment." They respond, "I did." "Okay, then, that's a good reason for which to stop, but remember, you're not always going to *feel* every little thing that happens, just like we don't *feel* every single thing that happens in our everyday lives. Does that make sense?" They reply, "Yes." And I continue.

"You must begin with **one** single fully engaged **honest** moment; it will lead you to the next, and so on. If you continue to the next moment, after your first moment was created on a false premise, or a weak foundation, or a half-truth, then what you have left is also going to be false, weak, or a half-truth. Your first moment is your foundation for creating or creating again. But you must trust your process and your impulses because you aren't always going to feel every little thing. Remember, you can't feel your way through acting, much to everyone's surprise. You must simply **actively participate** in each moment. Sometimes you'll feel something, sometimes you won't; or if we do feel something, we don't recognize it, or even know what it is, but we go on breathing and living. But you will always know when you are present and grounded in *creating again* the **environment**, and living with the character's **physiological attributes**, and being pro-active with the character's **action-based motivations** – all these you will know, and when you do, you just keep going … and don't look back. Just go, go, go!" "So I guess what you're saying is that even if I don't feel something I just need to be engaged anyway until the next **honest impulse** happens." "Yes."

•••

You will know when your actors are in the moment and can sustain the connection when, after the scene or performance is over, they find it a bit difficult to characterize what they've done. After minutes or hours of remaining in a subjective place, it is logical that it would take a bit of time to get back to a more objective place in their mind. You should also know from having experienced the results of their work, but the intangibles sometimes can get in the way.

•••

You will know it when you see it: the actors will know it when they *live* it.

PART III
METHODS

10

SYNTHESIZING INTERNAL PROCESS WITH EXTERNAL TECHNIQUE: LEARNING THE SECRET LANGUAGE, AND REPETITION

In far too many training programs, the synthesis of internal process with external technique is left to the actor to figure out on his or her own, usually *after* the actors have long left the training programs. This is a significant failure on the part of many programs. Our job as trainers is to finish what we have started; our job is to guide the actors toward as many methods, techniques, and solutions as possible, as well as allow and encourage the development of synthesis. At the very least, we should begin the attempts at synthesis *prior* to the actor leaving the program(s) of study.

The exhaustive work of masters such as Constantin Stanislavski, Uta Hagen, and Sanford Meisner is the foundation for most, if not all, actor training in internal process and dramatic technique. It is important to separate the two, but I also believe in guiding the actor toward a synthesis of the two, merging the **internal** personal *process* with the **external** technical *work*. This can be addressed as a capstone-styled project toward the end of the formal training, or it can be a final section of each and every component of the work along the way. For example, in a beginning acting class the final project can be a comprehensive scene that encompasses the majority of the work covered in the course of the semester, year, or workshop. In the one-semester freshman voice and movement course that I have taught, the first half of the semester is all voice work combined with Alexander technique; the second half of the term is spent working on an Alexander-Standard American-activity monologue project. The actors' challenge is to combine the Alexander technique with activities for the character, as they speak using a Standard American dialect. The singular, isolated goal of this work is deceptively simple for each of the actors, and they all find it daunting to amalgamate the creative with the analytical as they attempt to **move** utilizing the Alexander technique primary orders, **speak** Standard American from beginning to end, and **personate** the character.

In the voice and movement course, I also introduce my formwork, which I will detail in Chapter Thirteen. The formwork developed out of desperation two decades ago, when I discovered that the student actors weretnot synthesizing the Alexander technique into their acting on stage and in their acting coursework. I took what Jim Hancock, one of my graduate school mentors, taught me in one of our movement courses and gave it an additional twist. The formwork encourages the actors to keep the Alexander primary orders in mind, or keep them "alive," when speaking text and moving. It has always been important for me to guide my actors toward a synthesis of everything they are learning. And what I've learned through the years is that actors need the synthesizing to be a part of the work; they need processes, or practical tools, that point the way and assist them.

Keeping this in mind might be helpful: voice work is internal, while speech work is external; the Alexander technique is internal, while the Laban (movement) work is external; process monologues are internal and acting styles work is external. Your job is to find ways, methods, and tools to help your actors assimilate everything they've learned.

Most final projects in the Ole Miss Theatre acting studio courses are comprehensive, specifically-defined, and encourage a synthesis of the semester's work, whether it is in the Sophomore Acting Studio with Samuel Beckett scenes, or in the BFA Acting Studio with either Chekhov or Shakespearean scenes, depending on the spring semester. (The Chekhov synthesizes the classic comedy styles spring semester work and the Shakespearean scene synthesizes the classic dramatic styles spring semester training, which alternate from year to year.) For the BFA students, the exercises that layer the character's voice, physicality, speech, and psychological gestures are a final step for all scenework in the studio. These exercises can be tedious, but they reinforce the importance of discipline, analysis, and mastery of the art form.

•••

When synthesizing any of your work with the actors, it is important to learn how to read the **physical and facial signals**, the secret language, if you will, and differentiate what is superfluous, or affectation, from what an honest message looks like. I digress here for a reason: in late 2009, my sister, Virginia, to whom I was very close, passed away, and I am the one who found her in her apartment hours after she had passed on. I was thinking about this today as I drove by her (then) apartment, driving the car I inherited from her, and my hand impulsively covered my mouth, and I said to myself, "Stop it!" In that moment, when my hand impulsively covered my mouth, I realized that my body was speaking to me. That external gesture was an outward expression of what was happening deep inside my psyche, my heart, and my spirit. I had been suppressing, pushing down, and swallowing every honest impulse that pointed to what desperately needed attention. Up until then, I had not been paying much attention to the signals my physical being was giving me. I started listening, and the real healing followed and will probably be with me for some time; it's a process. Just like our personal experiences in life are a process, so goes the art of learning how to mirror life itself.

All humans are open books, and if you learn how to *read* them you learn the secret language. Most of us grew up learning about body language, which is a major part of what I call a secret language; the rest is a mix of recognizing psychological signals, physiological messages, and vocal/speech rhythms and patterns. I view learning this secret language as crucial to successful actor training and paramount to guiding actors toward synthesizing their training. We mentors of actors must learn the difference between affectation and valid non-verbal expression, the difference between a sigh and fear, between timidity and momentary apprehension, the difference between frustration and rage, the difference between exceptional acting and intermittently brilliant neuroses. Sometimes the measure of difference is miniscule, and an intangible conundrum ensues that we must address, resolve, or ignore for the time being. As example: Jamal, a young actor in the studio bounces his knee every time he is seated, whether acting a character or being himself. This has been a challenge for several years now, and he continues to bounce his knee. During the synthesis work, if this habitual movement cannot be settled, we must find a way to allow Jamal to incorporate the distracting knee bounce into the scene and give it purpose. Once the habit has purpose, we might be able to address it as a part of the character, actualizing the habit and merging it with the character. By transferring this habit to the character, Jamal will have an opportunity to objectify the behavior and create some distance; the distancing will take the pressure off Jamal and place it on the character he is developing. If successful, we have helped Jamal pull this annoying habit from a hidden *internal* habitat to an open *external* locale. As Jamal addresses the character's concerns and physicality, he will be addressing one of his obstacles. One of his personal challenges has not merely been addressed but remedied. Jamal will recognize his progress and apply this experience to other challenges along the way. I believe learning and utilizing this language of human nature is the key to breaking through to the actors' power source, to their distinctive mode of communication.

•••

Methodical, practical, targeted, and purposeful repetition is the key to synthesizing internal process and external technique. Just like repetition (or *reps*) is fundamental when training dancers, musicians, athletes, and anything that demands practice, repetition is essential when training the mind/body relationship and the consummate expression of an actor.

Don't hesitate to make scheduled repetition of difficult exercises a significant part of the training. Without repetition your students will never become mentally and physically familiar with each new training challenge they confront. With repetition comes familiarity, and we all know the old adage – *practice makes perfect*. Although the simple truth of this adage has become clichéd, it shouldn't keep us from making use of its practical advice. This is one instance where over-thinking or over-intellectualizing the work can trip us (mentors) up, just like over-analyzing can trip up an actor. A simple, common sense practice like repetition can go a long way to create a stronger foundation for actors. It will also allow a training actor to enduringly internalize your training. They will carry your work with them forever, if it is something familiar to them, if it has come to reside in a safe and well-known place in their being. Long after their work in your studio, they will turn to your training, especially when they find themselves in need of reassurance. This is also why I believe that most working actors are *trained* actors, as opposed to people who got lucky or had connections or were athletes prior to acting, or were reality television stars prior to acting. Methodical, practical, targeted, and purposeful repetition is the key to *successfully* synthesizing internal process and external technique.

Although it is rarely seen as a synthesizing tool, one should not overlook improvisation as a means for marrying honest impulse with technique. Viola Spolin's great methods as a trainer, director, and coach, known as "theatre games" are published in her book *Improvisation for the Theater.* Her useful exercises, as a final part of your course or studio work, can be a sure-fire method for making the process of synthesis second nature. Theatre games can help externalize your work and allow a true integration, since each improvisational action naturally derives from a spontaneous, honest impulse. It will be fun and provide your actors with something to hold on to.

Actors need reassurance. All of us need reassurance from time to time, but this is particularly true of actors because of the highly subjective nature of their work. They need something to hold onto long after their training. As they embark on their careers, they will be on their own and it will be your work with them that they will turn to for solace, counsel, and guidance in a career that often leaves them very much alone.

•••

It is your work that will give them the strength and confidence to move forward with courage and assertion.

11

THE STUDIO FORMAT

The studio format is what we (at Ole Miss Theatre) have coined the **3-teacher-team-taught** process of training our sophomores and BFA Studio actors. The **philosophy** of the studio format in both actor-training studios is to guide and train our undergraduate actors, who have juried into the studios, through a well-planned, integrated, and comprehensive acting studio experience. The **rationale** is that the students will be *guided* toward a *synthesis* of the training they receive in voice, speech, movement, and acting so that by the end of their training they will know, kinesthetically and intellectually, how to approach text and character during the rehearsal process on stage or as personal preparation for camera work.

The term *jury* is used in music departments; it is, for all practical purposes, a formal audition process. Our juries consist of a timed audition consisting of three monologues: one contemporary (assigned) dramatic, one contemporary comedic, and one classical; one minute each for a total audition time of three minutes. All male actors perform the same contemporary dramatic monologue, which they need to cut to no longer than one minute; all female actors perform the same contemporary dramatic monologue, which they need to cut to no longer than one minute. Freshmen jury for admittance into the Sophomore Acting Studio; sophomores jury for admittance into the BFA Acting Studio. The assigned monologues for freshmen are different from the assigned sophomore monologues.

HOW GUIDED **SYNTHESIS** WORKS IN THE STUDIO:

Here are two examples of how the faculty work together to integrate their respective specialties in the studio. The first example involves scenework and the second occurs during the process monologue work, using a working sample session from Chapter Two.

Scenework

The actors in the studio are working on Shaw scenes.

The voice and speech professor: works on well-grounded power resonance and provides an IPA Received Pronunciation (RP) review.

The movement professor: works on a review of the Alexander technique principles and application (which help the actors achieve George Bernard Shaw's "divine normal").

The acting professor: stresses the importance of incorporating what the voice and speech and movement professors are currently teaching or reviewing during the scenework steps. In fact, most of the assignment steps incorporate portions of the current voice, speech, and movement work. The movement and voice/speech professors are present during the (acting component) Shaw scenework and provide feedback, supporting what the acting professor is teaching and reminding the actors of their voice/speech and movement work.

Process Monologue

The acting professor will ask a student actor (we'll call her Mia) to be in the moment of extreme fear for her life (based on the demands of the text). She will work at that, and she will do her level best to live in that moment. Mia instinctively will, at some point during the exercise, hold her breath, because that is what people do when confronted with sheer terror. The problem for Mia is that she must speak most of the dialogue during the scene of sheer terror. Mia needs to breathe freely in order to deliver her lines, to allow the audience to hear, and to function as an actress of worth. Mia will need to modify her breathing, which instinctively is being told by her own "sense of reality in the moment" to hold her breath, thereby causing her to constrict her neck muscles, which will constrict her vocal mechanism. This is one of the conundrums of training actors: we work diligently to teach them complex techniques or processes, which they must then contradict.

During this working session, as the acting professor is working with the student:

1. The movement professor will step in and remind Mia of a principle they learned or reviewed earlier today.
2. The voice and speech professor will step in and take one minute to make a physical and breath-related adjustment that Mia immediately responds to.
3. The acting professor can move forward and the goal is for Mia to have learned how to synthesize the actor-training work for herself.

We have taught her to synthesize the work. And the guidance provided by all three professors, although at first daunting, is actually a safety net that allows the students to risk failure or foolishness. We allow the ego to momentarily retreat, allowing Mia the freedom to risk and therefore learn.

NOTE: The studio format works best when all three professors are in agreement pedagogically and philosophically. The studio format professors need to be willing to listen to new and improved methods suggested by any of the three professors who will achieve the agreed-upon goal (or goals.) We constantly and consistently "tweak" our curriculum, weekly lesson plans, and methods. We learn, from year to year, what works best, as our students evolve from year to year and, more importantly, as their needs evolve from year to year.

•••

The studio format functions in a liberal arts setting, no differently from how it works in a conservatory. The list of challenges or possible obstacles begins with philosophical and pedagogical unity amongst the teaching faculty.

1. There must be universal respect for the student actor, or put in other words, the studio format will not succeed in a faculty-centered department or school. The department or school must be student-centered. At its core, the studio format *is* student-centered; it was created with **student-centered concerns** in mind.

2. The studio team teachers must respect each other as professionals and be willing to adjust (slightly) their own style, form, and content from time to time. The success of the studio format is highly dependent on the evolution of the team-taught curriculum from year to year. This is more difficult than it sounds; it demands efficient and well organized, committed faculty. I'm sure you ask your actors this question regularly: "What did you learn today?" It is a regular question at the end of the studio day. "What did you learn this semester?" is also asked at the end of the term, immediately followed by "Give us suggestions; what would improve the transference, or communication, of this semester's work?" Student input gives them (the actors) a stake in the work, both while training and long after they have left and are deep into their careers. (Last year, one of the BFA actors in the studio complained on Facebook about something regarding the rigors of the studio training; they promptly received five replies from working alums, scolding them for laziness, arrogance, and short-sightedness.)

3. Proper time slot lengths need to be scheduled; and it can sometimes be difficult to find approval from university, school, or college curriculum committees. For example, the percentage of studio time should be divided as such: 10 percent movement; 10 percent voice; 10 percent speech; 70 percent acting. Why is more emphasis placed on the acting component? Because the acting component is where the synthesis takes place and synthesis can be a time-consuming process.

4. The studio format team teachers must be willing to work toward success, which at times includes long hours. The time commitment is a difficult reality connected to the use of the studio format. Most theatre instructors, teachers, professors, or coaches are already overworked; asking them to put in additional hours demands a commitment from the professors and/or some type of compensation. In these budget-conscious times, it usually means "a selfless commitment."

•••

A typical week in the **Sophomore Acting Studio** is as follows:

Monday
1 – 2pm	Character or Shaw/Targeting work
2 – 2:40	Voice/Speech
2:45 – 4pm	Acting

Tuesday
11 – 12:15pm	Movement

Wednesday
1 – 1:30pm	Movement
1:30 – 2:30pm	Voice/Speech
2:35 – 4pm	Acting

A typical week in the **BFA Acting Studio** is as follows:

Tuesday
1 – 1:35pm	Movement
1:35 – 2:30pm	Voice/Speech
2:35 – 4pm	Acting

Thursday
11 – 12:15pm	Movement
1 – 2:30pm	Voice/Speech
2:35 – 4pm	Acting

All three teachers are present for all evaluated rounds of work in movement, voice, and speech. "Evaluated rounds of work" implies that the student actors will receive written feedback from all three professors for second and final rounds of work. All three professors are present for all acting component work.

•••

The studio format is a godsend for determined actors; it isn't for the actor who has a passing interest in the art form. As demanding as the studio format is for the professors or instructors, it can be twice as demanding for the student (or training) actor. The commitment of time in the studio is significant; the demands of rehearsal time outside the studio are absolutely essential. Actors who want to keep up with the work in a studio format acting studio must commit to the habit of rehearsing; actors who want to excel in the studio know that they will need to devote themselves almost exclusively to the work in and outside the studio. Educators may object to rigorous conservatory-style training or something as intense as the studio format, on the basis that students have other coursework to consider. I understand that argument. However, our most successful BFA (studio format) actors are also musical theatre majors and/or are also enrolled in the Ole Miss Honors College.

•••

If you want results, this is one sure-fire way to achieve excellence and achieve your actor-training goals.

12

THE CHARACTER PROFILE PAPER

CHARACTER PROFILE PAPERS

A minimum two-page, maximum three-page typewritten paper due at first and second rounds of work. The paper should contain four sections, each separated into a *textual research sub-section* and a *choices sub-section*. *Voice*: textual research (*quotes*), *choices; speech*: textual research (*quotes*), *choices; physical characteristics*: textual research (*quotes*), *choices; psychological* or *personality profile*: textual research (*quotes*), *choices*. TEXTUAL RESEARCH PAPER IS DUE AT FIRST ROUND. TEXTUAL RESEARCH <u>AND</u> CHOICES PAPER IS DUE AT SECOND ROUND. (*At the final round, you will be evaluated on your attempt to portray the character you have profiled.*) <u>**Your CPP must be accompanied by a rehearsal schedule, detailing assignment steps and assigned voice and movement charts.**</u>

This is what appears in all of my acting classes and acting studio syllabi. The character profile paper (CPP) continues the process of linking the mind to the body; it will heighten the actors' research and interpretation skills. It requires that the actor read the entire script, not merely the scene that will be acted. It requires the actor to seek out material (**textual research**) in the *entire* text that relates to the character's **voice, speech, physicality,** and **personality** in the form of actual quotes spoken by the character or other characters in the play or screenplay. (Sometimes the playwright's or screenwriter's instructions can be included, which would be logical, but the point is for the actor to see beyond the mere instructions, or stage directions, to seek out nuance and create a character only he or she can create.)

After the actors have presented their scene for a first round, and continue their rehearsals in preparation for a second round presentation, each actor writes a brief **personal analysis (in the form of choices)** for each of the four character profiles: **voice, speech, physicality**, and **personality**. This encourages the actor to make intelligent choices based on the text; the actors will also retain an additional boost of confidence knowing their "interpretation" choices are the best they can be. All too often actors make choices that have little or no connection to the text, which weakens the writing, the performance, and, in the end, the production.

BFA ACTING STUDIO

Ole Miss Theatre   Names of 3 professors:

CHARACTER PROFILE PAPER   *Sample Template*

Name: your name here   <<<< notice

PLAY: ROMES 'N JULES by Elvira Sims Doe   <<<< notice
ROLE: Jules   <<<< notice

Your CPP must be accompanied by a rehearsal schedule, detailing assignment steps.

VOICE   (See Voice and Speech syllabus.)
Textual Research: **Quotes** from the entire text, with minimal explanation.
for Round One
Choices: Based on my research of Jules' voice, I have concluded that....
(*at least a long paragraph*) **Add for Round Two and include Textual Research**

SPEECH   (See Voice and Speech syllabus.)
Textual Research: **Quotes** from the entire text, with minimal explanation.
for Round One
Choices: Based on my research of Jules' speech, I have concluded that....
(*at least a long paragraph*) **Add for Round Two and include Textual Research**

MOVEMENT / PHYSICALITY (See Movement syllabus in the Spring term.)
Textual Research: **Quotes** from the entire text, with minimal explanation.
for Round One
Choices: Based on my research of Jules' movements, I have concluded that....
(*at least a long paragraph*) **Add for Round Two and include Textual Research**
Apply LMA Concepts. (*For example: How will you use the LMA to
physicalize your choices?*)

PSYCHOLOGICAL/PERSONALITY TRAITS
Textual Research: **Quotes** from the entire text, with minimal explanation.
for Round One
Choices: Based on my research of Jules' psychological profile, I have
concluded that.... (*at least a long paragraph*) **Add for Round Two and
include Textual Research**

As you can see from this sample template, the first round CPP is all textual research (mostly quotes from the text, with accompanying page numbers) and the second round CPP is the textual research plus their choices for each of the four categories. The reasoning behind not including the choices in the first round paper is that it allows the actors more rehearsal time and feedback from the instructors prior to making choices (personal analysis), thus discouraging the actors from making final choices until sufficient textual research and rehearsal has taken place.

Once the CPP is complete, the actors have, in writing, a map for their character's journey; their character profile is accessible and can be used during rehearsals as reference. Actors need guidance, as we all know, and in place of the non-existent director, during their studio scenework rehearsals away from the studio, the actors can confidently move forward with their exploration and choices.

The final CPP is this second round paper they have completed. Why not have the actors turn in their final paper at their final (and third) round performance? Because between the second round presentation and the final round performance, the actors need to focus on giving shape to their character development choices and move beyond the research, analysis, and paperwork; in other words, shift from "analysis" work to "realizing" their choices. Simply put, for the final round performance, the actors need to get out of their heads and into their bodies. (Notice the use of vocabulary when referring to first and second round **presentations** and final round **performances**. This is to separate the final result from the developmental work.)

Here now are three actual character profile papers, which I am using with my students' permission. These character profile papers were written by Taylor Ragan, Paige Mattox, and Jake Johnson, BFA Studio alums.

BFA Acting Studio   **date**

Ole Miss Theatre   Names of three professors

Character Profile Paper   Name: Taylor Ragan

PLAY: Tartuffe by Moliere
ROLE: Elmire

VOICE
TEXTUAL RESEARCH
-"Please Wait. We can't keep up with you." (pleading) p. 21
-"And all for *my* unworthy sake." p. 63
-"I need you to be frank with me." p. 64 (demanding)
-"Don't squeeze so hard! You'll squash my hand!" p. 64
-"And in *flagrante rendez-vous* Conducted in full view of you you'll see him at it."
p. 82
-"(Whispers) That'll be him. Take up your post. Don't let him see you or all is lost."
p. 84
-"Shut the door and check, check carefully." p. 84
-" I was afraid for *you*, I mean—" p. 84
-"Why then Monsieur, it's plain enough you don't know women, or the clues we give,
the secret code we use." p. 85
-"What did you understand by that? What was I really driving at?" p. 85
-"Didn't I more or less declare: 'I want you all and not a share!'?" p. 85
-"These words from *you*, the one I love, The woman I've been dreaming of, they
course like honey through each vein." p. 86

CHOICES
    Elmire's use of voice is fairly strong. She does not falter when she speaks and
she is not quiet or timid, and her voice reflects that. She is a strong woman with
very clear ideas and opinions. Her voice resides in her chest and is a little deeper
and sometimes sultry, so that she can not only command, but also seduce and
control. When angry, she does not raise her voice so much as she controls her
volume and speaks with an unnerving clam. Like most women are depicted of
the time, Elmire has a few lines where she suffers from hysterics, but that is very
rare. When she is with Tartuffe, she utilizes a very manipulative voice that flows
and oozes as she speaks with inflection and emotion.

SPEECH

TEXTUAL RESEARCH

-"Too good, too kind, too Christian." p. 63

-"I need you to be frank with me." p. 64 (imperative)

-"Don't squeeze so hard! You'll squash my hand!" p. 64

-"Ugly scene." P. 69 "nasty scene." p. 84

-"And in *flagrante rendez-vous* conducted in full view of you- you'll see him at it." p. 82

-"(whispers) That'll be him. Take up your post. Don't let him see you or all is lost." p. 84

-"More..." p. 84

-"Remember last time, and Damis-- ?" p. 84

-" I was afraid for *you*, I mean—" p. 84

-"all's well that ends well, eh?" p. 84

-"It's clear we're really ripe for sin: we turn you down—you know you're in." p. 85

-"These words from *you*, the one I love, The woman I've been dreaming of, they course like honey through each vein." P. 86

-"MY!" p. 87

CHOICES

Throughout the play, Elmire often repeats certain words or phrases especially when she is with Tartuffe. It's almost as she's speaking absent mindedly in order to think of the next clever thing to say to him. When she speaks, her language flows into long paragraphs meaning she has a lot to say. IN order to make a point, she emphasizes certain words such as "you." She speaks in French sometimes. There are many times that she is caught off guard by Tartuffe and her speech either is cut off or trails off. She exclaims quite frequently when surprised, and tries to slow Tartuffe's advances with questions and flowery analogies. Her rhythm lengthens to let the syllables and vowels ooze when she is being seductive, but other wise, she speaks at a moderate space with very strong and clear diction.

MOVEMENT/ PHYSICALITY
TEXTUAL RESEARCH
-"We can't keep up with you." p. 21
-"We're alone." p. 63
-"I was afraid for *you*, I mean—" p. 84
-"You saw yourself how hard I tried to calm him, and stop the leak." P. 84
-"I can be bolder now, and start to open up my amorous heart, and hasten to re-ciprocate your love—or maybe I should wait...?" p. 84
-"Why then Monsieur, it's plain enough you don't know women, or the clues we give, the secret code we use." p. 85
-"Some small resistance we must make, if only for our honor's sake." p. 85
-"I am—*mistrustful* nonetheless: Why would you drop into my lap? How do I know it's not a trap? Let me be frank: I don't see why you wouldn't stoop to tell a lie." p. 86
-"My goodness what a nasty cough!" p. 87
-Oh, no, this phlegm is here to stay." p. 88
-"It seems I've no alternative but to give in, so in I'll give." p. 88

CHOICES
   Because she is a strong and confident woman, Elmire moves through her spine. She utilizes rotary factor when she is attempting to be seductive. She mostly has strong weight, but is a little more light weight when she is attempting to re-move herself from Tartuffe's advances. Most her movements are very direct and intentional, and she even utilizes some carving while trying to seduce Tartuffe.

PSYCHOLOGICAL
TEXTUAL RESEARCH
-"That's because *I* don't want you to. These antics chill me to the core." p. 21
-"(whispers) That'll be him. Take up your post. Don't let him see you or all is lost." p. 84
-"You know he really frightened me—I was afraid for you, I mean—" p. 84
-"I should have said it was a lie" p. 84
-"People will talk, they always do—" p. 84
-"I can be bolder now, and start to open up my amorous heart, and hasten to re-ciprocate your love—or maybe I should wait...?" p. 84
-"Why then Monsieur, it's plain enough you don't know women, or the clues we give, the secret code we use." p. 85

-"Some small resistance we must make, if only for our honor's sake." p. 85

-"Didn't I more or less declare: 'I want you all and not a share!'?" p. 85

-"I am—*mistrustful* nonetheless: Why would you drop into my lap? How do I know it's not a trap? Let me be frank: I don't see why you wouldn't stoop to tell a lie." p. 86

-"Won't Heaven frown upon us though?" p. 87

-"It seems I've no alternative but to give in, so in I'll give." p. 88

CHOICES

Psychologically, Elmire is a very smart person. She is well aware from the beginning that Tartuffe is a fraud. She utilizes different tactics to try and show her husband the truth, by talking, pleading, and even tricking Tartuffe. When she wants to be, she can be very manipulative as is shown when she tries to encourage Tartuffe's advances to prove his hypocrisy. It is obvious throughout the play that the wheels are always spinning in her head, but there are no real descriptions of her inner character, so most of her psychology is deduced from her actions. She is very womanly, as is described by her flirting games with Tartuffe and she fully understands what makes her beautiful and how to use it to get her way. She also understands men very well and knows how to use what they want against them.

Taylor Ragan

Moliere Scene **Rehearsal Schedule/Log (with scene partner)** – to accompany CPP

First scene of comedy styles semester

Ole Miss Theatre - BFA Studio

Steps – assigned from class to class throughout first rounds:

1. Chair Work (lifting the lines off of the page, introducing the characters)
2. Moving on every line (gesture, cross, sit, etc.)
3. Moving after every line
4. Moving before every line
5. Combining the movement and moving during, after, or before every line
6. 2 min of the scene with form work
7. Move the entire scene with free form (formwork)
8. Change the delivery and movement of lines each line (cross frantically, sit down calmly, etc.) Perform scene again and allow arms to become a part of it.
9. Make choices

February 6 (5:30-6:00)

Step 1: Chair work

February 9 (3:00-4:30)

Step 2: Move on every line

Step 3: Move after every line

Step 4: Move before every line

Step 5: Move during, after, or before every line

February 12 (11:00-12:00)

Step 6: 2 min of scene with form work

Step 7: Move entire scene with free form

February 13 (5:30-7:00)

Step 8: Change the delivery and movement. Perform scene a 2nd time with arms

Step 9: Make choices

Block scene

BFA Acting Studio   **date**

Ole Miss Theatre   Names of three professors

Paige Mattox

Character Profile Paper

BFA Performance Studies (BFA Acting Studio)

Play: *Angels in America (Part One)* by Tony Kushner

Character: Harper

VOICE

Textual Research: "...things are collapsing, lies surfacing, systems of defense giving way..."(p17) "I'm not safe here you see. Things aren't right with me. Weird stuff happens." (p17) "And if I do have emotional problems it's from living with you." (p27) "I have emotional problems. I took too many pills." (p31) "Joe will be so angry. I promised him. No more pills....Valium. I take Valium. Lots of Valium." (p32) "The world. Finite. Terribly, terribly...Well..."(p33) "I have to go now, get back, something just...fell apart. Oh God I feel so sad..."(p34) "No, no, not that, that's Utah talk, Mormon talk, I hate it, Joe, tell me, say it..." (p40) "No. Yes. No. Yes. Get away from me. Now we both have a secret." (p41) "I feel better, I do, I...feel better. There are ice crystals in my lungs, wonderful and sharp." (p101) "We'll mend together. That's what we'll do. We'll mend." (p103)

Choices: Harper wears her internal processes on her sleeve and, more importantly, in her voice. While she tries to put on a happy ("pretend happy"), light façade of buoyant inflection and bright pitches, this "system of defense" gives way to betray the undercurrent of fear and collapse that turns her inward. In these moments, her voice becomes soft and nearly monotone, as she is so concerned with the flashing images of destruction and pain behind her eyes that the external world registers very little. Harper, though weak and soft in her more tender moments, is not without her strength. Quite the contrary, she is a strong woman who has allowed herself to be broken, and contributed a good deal to that herself since she doesn't believe her own strength. Consequently, when that strength manifests itself in a powerful, barking, tearing outburst of vocal force, she is usually scared into her place of barely voiced murmurings – as if afraid anything louder would cause the truth to rend the world around her.

SPEECH

Textual Research: *"She is listening to the radio and talking to herself, as she often does."*(p16) "I'm not safe here you see. Things aren't right with me. Weird stuff happens." (p17) "...maybe my life is really fine, maybe Joe loves me and I'm only crazy thinking otherwise, or maybe not, maybe it's worse than I even know, maybe...I want to know, maybe I don't..."(p18) "No change. Why?" (p23) "None. One. Three. Only three." (p24) "Joe will be so angry. I promised him. No more pills....Valium. I take Valium. Lots of Valium." (p32) "I'm not addicted. I don't believe in addiction." (p32) "No, no, not that, that's Utah talk, Mormon talk, I hate it, Joe, tell me, say it..." (p40) "No. Yes. No. Yes. Get away from me. Now we both have a secret." (p41)

Choices: Harper's speech mimics her internal thought process very closely, with all its starts, stops, and disjointed phrases. She usually either speaks in fragments of a few words, or allows her continually spiraling psyche to surface in her words and pours out a deluge of psychological word vomit. Her biggest "weapon", if you could call it that, in the use of her voice is the pacing – either slow, deliberate, and continual, or running at such a rapid crescendo that she can barely get out what she wants to say. Similarly, she either uses almost no pitch or power, or emphasizes a point with a dramatic variety of both – usually at critical moments where her walls are crumbling and she's making a last ditch effort to patch up the leaks.

MOVEMENT/PHYSICALITY

Textual Research: "...things are collapsing, lies surfacing, systems of defense giving way..."(p17) "I'm not safe here you see. Things aren't right with me. Weird stuff happens." (p17) "People are like planets, you need a thick skin. Things get to me. Joe stays away and now..." (p18) "Its the price of rootlessness. Motion sickness. The only cure: to keep moving." (p18) "I have emotional problems. I took too many pills." (p31) "Joe will be so angry. I promised him. No more pills....Valium. I take Valium. Lots of Valium." (p32) "The world. Finite. Terribly, terribly...Well..."(p33) "I have to go now, get back, something just...fell apart. Oh God I feel so sad..."(p34) "I dream that you batter away at me till all my joints come apart, like wax, and I fall into pieces. It's like a punishment." (p37) "No. Yes. No. Yes. Get away from me. Now we both have a secret." (p41) "...I loved it that she was always wrong, always doing something wrong, like one step out of step." (p53)

Choices: Harper is a very still person. She generally feels as though she is standing, on tip toe, on the edge of a cliff so high that she can't see the bottom, imbuing her movements with a deliberate sense of not upsetting the delicate balance that she has created in her life. However, Harper has reached a point in her life where that delicate balance is collapsing, and when she finds herself over the edge, that same strength that occasionally lashes out in her voice does the same in her body, bringing unexpected bursts of powerful, barely controlled, desperate movement in moments where she feels cornered or out of control. Despite being, at the core, a very still person, Harper has a habit of nervously "playing with" her right foot, and rubbing her right cheek against her right shoulder in moments where she just doesn't know what else to do. When attacked, however, her best and most frequently used defense is to "play possum", in a way, and freeze entirely while the storm batters away at her crumbling barricades.

PSYCHOLOGICAL

Textual Research: *"She is listening to the radio and talking to herself, as she often does."*(p16) "People who are lonely, people left alone, sit talking nonsense to the air, imagining..."(p16) "...things are collapsing, lies surfacing, systems of defense giving way..."(p17) "I'm not safe here you see. Things aren't right with me. Weird stuff happens." (p17) "People are like planets, you need a thick skin. Things get to me. Joe stays away and now..." (p18) "...maybe my life is really fine, maybe Joe loves me and I'm only crazy thinking otherwise, or maybe not, maybe it's worse than I even know, maybe...I want to know, maybe I don't..."(p18) "Well happy enough! Pretend-happy. That's better than nothing."(p23) "No change. Why?" (p23) "None. One. Three. Only three." (p24) "This is a good time. For me to make a baby." (p27) "Then they went on to a program about holes in the ozone layer. Over Antarctica. Skin burns, birds go blind, icebergs melt. The world's coming to an end." (p28) "And if I do have emotional problems it's from living with you." (p27) "I have emotional problems. I took too many pills." (p31) "I'm not *addicted*. I don't believe in addiction." (p32) "It's terrible. Mormons are not supposed to be addicted to anything. I'm a Mormon....In my church we don't believe in homosexuals."(p32) "Joe's a very normal man, he...Oh God. Oh God. He...Do homos take, like, lots of long walks?" (p33) "It just seemed the kind of thing a mentally deranged sex-starved pill-popping housewife would do."(p36) "I dream that you batter away at me till all my joints come apart, like wax, and I fall into pieces. It's like a punishment." (p37) "God won't talk to me. I have to make up people to talk to me." (p40) "No, no, not that, that's Utah talk, Mormon talk, I hate it, Joe, tell me, say it..." (p40) "In the whole entire world, you are the only person, the only person I love or have ever loved. And I love you terribly. Terribly. That's what's so awfully, irreducibly real. I can make up anything but I can't dream that away." (p50) "...I loved it that she was always wrong, always doing something wrong, like one step out of step." (p53) "We'll mend together. That's what we'll do. We'll mend." (p103)

Choices: The facts about Harper are fairly simple. She's a valium addict with a husband she believes to be gay, who spends most of her time alone at her house (owing to her agoraphobia) speaking to her hallucinations or fearing a man under her bed with a knife. It would be very easy to dismiss her, then, as a crazy woman, plain and simple. And in many ways, Harper IS textbook crazy – but that's not nearly the whole picture. At her very heart of hearts, Harper is a strong woman, who could easily be self-sufficient and sane. But her complicated attachment to Joe, as well as the slow, steady self-destruction of her faith, has turned Harper instead into a self-proclaimed martyr, of sorts. She hurts because of the rift between her and Joe, and thinks that this hurt will show how much she actually does love him – in a way, she thrives off of it, off the idea that things are falling apart. Which, to a degree, they are. This means, though, she is completely taken aback and most thrown in moments where things go RIGHT – when Joe is tender, and they find that "buddy" moment, is destroys every defense she may have built up while believing that things were bad. She does love Joe, completely and entirely – as she puts it, it's the one thing she can't "dream away", the one thing she has absolutely no control over, and it terrifies her. She is a living contradiction to herself, hiding her truth away under layers upon layers of misleading quirks, while at the same time holding her internal everything so close to the surface that it can't help but burst through impulsively and erratically.

BFA Acting Studio

Jake Johnson
3/17/15
Joe Turner Cantu

Shakespeare Monologue Final Round
Play: *Hamlet*
Role: Hamlet
Author: William Shakespeare

VOICE
Research: "Must I remember? Why, she would hang on him
As if increase of appetite had grown
By what it fed on: and yet, within a month,—
Let me not think on't" – Hamlet (Act 1 Scene 2)
"Mother, you have my father much offended" – Hamlet (Act 3 Scene 4)
"You are the queen, your husband's brother's wife/ And would it were not so, you are
my mother" – Hamlet. (Act 3 Scene 4)
"Fie on't! Oh Fie!" (Act 1 Scene 2)
"There is nothing either good or bad, but thinking it makes it so" (Act 2 Scene 2)

Choices: My voice is soft but sharp. Precise and yet still gentle overall. Moments of
rough sounds come from my voice during serious moments of frustration. I am a
Prince so I obviously sound like royalty when I use my voice. I, Hamlet, use more of
my upper register than Jake does. A simile for my voice would be like a soft blanket
holding a child. Vocally I use a large range in volume, often talking down to a 3 of the
volume scale and at times, reaching to a 9. I feel that I like to hear myself speak when
I am in a deep depression.

SPEECH
Research: "A little more than kin and less than kind." – Hamlet (Act 1 Scene 2)
"By what it fed on: and yet, within a month" (Act 1 Scene 2)
"My father's brother; but no more like my father
Than I to Hercules" – Hamlet (Act 1 Scene 2)
"To be, or not to be: That is the question" (Act 3 Scene 1)
"There is nothing either good or bad, but thinking it makes it so" (Act 2 Scene 2)

Choices: I am a Prince, and this can be heard through the way I speak. I sound quite well-educated because I am in fact a smart educated man. I use inflection often and well to highlight images as I speak. I am a sad depressed man, which can be heard through the quality of my speech. I use consents very well and often stretch out vowels to emphasize sounds in certain words. A simile for my speech would be like a soaring bald eagle that lost his way.

PHYSICALITY
Research: "She married:-O' most wicked speed, to post with such dexterity to incestuous sheets!" – Hamlet (Act 1 Scene 2)
"But break my heart,—for I must hold my tongue" (Act 1 Scene 2)
"His Canon 'gainst self-slaughter! O God! O God! (Act 1 Scene 2)
"As if increase of appetite had grown" (Act 1 Scene 2)
"But two months dead" (Act 1 Scene 2)

Choices: I am in very good shape for my age. I feel that I am in my physical prime. I am comfortable with my body and this can be seen through the way in which I move. I am both sharp and smooth in my movements. I am a fairly direct person with moments of indirectness. I am a physically aligned human being. I feel that I may drink too much now since I am depressed about my uncle killing my father and marrying my mother. This alcoholism affects both my brain and my body. I am a very good swordsman, and this is a credit to how I am physically in my prime.

PSYCHOLOGY
Research:
"How weary, stale, flat, and unprofitable seem to me all the uses of this world!"- Hamlet (Act 1 Scene 2)
"*Indeed, my lord, you made me believe so*" – Ophelia(Act 3 Scene 1)
"*You should not have believed me...I loved you not*" – Hamlet(Act 3 Scene 1)
"*I was the more deceived*" – Ophelia (Act 3 Scene 1)
"*Hamlet, thou hast thy father much offended*"-Gertrude (Act 3 Scene 4)
"There is nothing either good or bad, but thinking it makes it so" (Act 2 Scene 2)

Choices: I am a horrifyingly brilliant and depressed individual. I loved my father who was killed by mine uncle, and now I have such a hatred for my mother, who has betrayed my father by marrying his murderer months after his death. I am suicidal. I would kill myself if I didn't have such a desire and hatred within me to have revenge on mine uncle. It is the only thing in this world keeping me going. As long as Claudius is alive, I will be alive. I will see him die, I will see to't that my mother loses her second husband. A husband that she never should have married. Mine Uncle, who I despise, he will die. A simile for my psychology would be like a boy who is being chased in the woods and can see with night-vision. Or like a badger stuck in a maze trying to claw his way out.

Words that needed clarification:

1. Fie – exclaimation used to express disgust or outrage

2. Hyperion – One of the Titans and the father of Helios, the sun-god.

3. Satyr – one of a class of lustful, drunken, woodland gods.

4. Niobe – a daughter of Tantalus and of either Dione, sister of Pelops and Broteas galled-bitterness, spitefulness, vindictiveness

Shakespeare Monologue: Rehearsal Log

Steps for Shakespeare:
1. Scansion and targeting
2. Pronunciation and meaning
3. Break at end of every Ten-Syllable line
4. Full stop at periods and colons.
5. Meter and meaning
6. Verse and movement

2/23/2015: I have first round tomorrow and I have scanned my monologue from Hamlet, the cliché "To be or not to be" monologue. I feel like if I am ever going to experiment with this monologue, now would be a perfect time to do it with this unit of work.

2/25/2015: I have second round tomorrow and I have now changed my monologue due to the nature of how overdone the "To be or not to be" is. I have now chosen to do the monologue "O' that this too too solid" that is in Act 1 scene 2, also from Hamlet. This monologue really spoke to me because of how crazy he talks in the beginning and then how much hatred he has for his mother toward the end of the monologue. I love my mother very much, but there is something appealing to me about playing a character who is truly livid at his mother for her actions, and rightfully so. I have gone through all the steps we have been given up to this point 1-4.

3/2/2015: Due to a snow day on Thursday, we will now be doing our second round tomorrow. I feel fairly confident in my monologue. I am still working on memorization because I changed my choice of monologue after first round.

3/5/2015: We had another snow day today, but I worked on my monologue with steps 5 and 6 today. I really found a lot of new things to play around with in this monologue. I really liked Joe's advice to let the text move me, and to not force emotion. I am glad he told me I was forcing because it didn't feel natural and obviously it wasn't at all. It is good to know when I am doing something incorrectly so I can have an opportunity to fix it.

3/15/2015: After a long spring break, I knew I needed to look over my lines again. I feel like it was a year since I last spoke them aloud, even though it was only ten days. I spent this evening re-memorizing and familiarizing myself with the textual and sub-textual information

3/16/2015: Tonight was the first night for the devised theatre company rehearsals, and wow do my knees hurt! I am now practicing my monologue at home and will continue to do so in the morning. I feel pretty confident about where I am with the piece but at the same time, I wish I could have done it before the break. The break caused me to lose a slight emotional connection to the text due to time away from it. Overall, I feel that I am ready to go tomorrow and I have really enjoyed this unit of work.

•••

Actors respond extremely well to their work on the character profile papers. After years of practice, the hope is that the actor will continue this type of research (text analysis and character profiling) within the regular rehearsal time frame when cast. Learning how to scan text and profile a character is also a plus at auditions, during the quick read, when the actor is called back for a role.

•••

The actor has a dependable tool and process for breathing life into the character, from the page to the stage, from the writer's words to on-camera work.

13

FORMING YOUR OWN STYLE: COMBINING NEW AND OLD METHODS

Actor-training, like anything else, evolves as the decades fly by. And we should thank our lucky stars that it does. It's only logical that students become mentors to their students, who in turn become mentors to a new generation, and so on. I honor my mentors every time I step into the acting studio to teach; my students honor me when their training becomes a vital part of their newfound success, whatever the profession. It is important for us to stay informed and move forward with our work; it is also important to know when something tried and true works quite well, thank-you-very-much. As I hope you've guessed by now, I do not believe there is only one best technique or method to training actors, but I do believe the teacher's attitude influences the success of the training. If the teacher's attitude is positive and nurturing in spirit, then most anything you teach will make an impact. If our attitude is less than positive, then how can we attain, or expect, positive results? To me, an abundance of negative energy goes against the grain of our pedagogical purpose. I don't believe in cynicism, as a general rule, and certainly not as a teaching aid. And, as I'm not a jaded person, I forge ahead with mustered energy, choosing to believe that I will make a difference …today. (Images of Pollyanna must be forming in your imagination.) I don't know any other way of approaching my work…not when young people, or any actors for that matter, are depending on me to guide them. So, I trust what I know and create new ways of addressing the task at hand, from one day to the next.

There is a strong argument for keeping up with ever-changing technology; this is particularly true for the future role of education in society. It is also true of actor-training, but to a lesser degree. For example, online or web-based courses are becoming the norm at countless colleges and universities in the world. And there are attempts to teach acting classes via the Internet. But, no matter the technological advancements in the coming decades, training in the performing arts demands live person-to-person interaction. The performing arts are experiential in nature; the student learning the particular artistic discipline must be able to experience it kinesthetically and emotionally in order for the art form to be absorbed by the mind, body, and spirit. There is no getting around this. That said, I believe we, as trainers, coaches, and directors of actors must adjust for, and to, our ever-changing students' needs. For example, I have noticed that **self-discipline**, **organizational skills**, and **problem-solving**, are increasingly lacking in our incoming freshmen classes in recent years. The absence of these learned skills reduces cognitive abilities and affects the students' abilities to move forward confidently. So, my teaching modules have had to adjust to this growing trend. I have had to address these lacking skills along with the planned curriculum. "Disciplining and organizing oneself" and "solving problems for oneself" have become naturally growing components in the teaching of the acting art form. Maybe this has always been the case, and what I have personally been experiencing as a teacher is an anomaly, but I don't think so. In fact, I believe this is a growing reality for all educators and trainers across the education spectrum. And, I believe it is a direct result of the increasing speed in technological advancements. All the more reason to stop, breathe, and be introspective, for ourselves and our students, from time to time. As far as this intangible aspect to teaching is concerned, I do have advice: trust your instincts. Listen to what your gut is telling you in the moment, and move forward confidently. This in itself will allow you to also listen to your surfacing methods and techniques, which will hopefully merge with your learned teaching techniques and methods. I tell myself almost every day that I am the one my students are facing and turning to, not my mentors; my mentors are not in the room. I am responsible. This, today, is my teaching; this, today, is what I have to contribute … joyfully.

We all learned from our mentors and we all eventually learn how to trust our instincts. Kristin Linklater learned from her mentor, Iris Warren, at the London Academy of Music and Dramatic Arts, and forged ahead with her Linklater Technique. As a teenager, Catherine Fitzmaurice learned from her mentor, Barbara Bunch, at Central School in London; she went on to study extensively worldwide and become a master of her field, voicework. Lee Strasburg and Sanford Meisner took Stanislavski's master teachings and gave it their own spin; Larry Silverberg continues Meisner's work to this day, and has added his touches to this great work.

I feel certain that I'm not espousing anything new here; we all take what we've learned and combine it with our own newfound methods of teaching, but I mention this because I am also aware that some of us teachers might lack the confidence to listen to our instincts. We are no different from the actors we train; I encourage us all to trust our instincts when confronting daily challenges.

When teaching in Arizona in the late 90s and early 2000s, I noticed that my students were experiencing difficulty applying the Alexander technique to their performances in the studio. Out of necessity, I took an exercise learned in graduate school and developed it into what I came to call **Formwork**, a "bridge" from the principles of the Alexander technique to authentic active movement while speaking complex text. Formwork assists actors with the synthesizing process. At first, I meant for it to be a one-time, one-class-day exercise; it was so successful, I began to add and embellish and eventually created a six-step movement exercise program detailed below:

FORMWORK
by Joe Turner Cantú

The word "Alexandered" is used to imply that the Alexander primary orders are engaged and flowing-constant. Alexander's primary orders are: neck lengthened; head forward and up; back widened.

1. *Form 1: On Back*: Flat back. One cycle with knees up; another cycle with legs extended. Arm movement "in form" (which needs to be modeled in person). One at a time. Alternating. Simultaneous.

2. *Form 2: Standing Alexandered*: Arm movements. One at a time. Alternating. Simultaneous.

3. *Cross Pattern 1*: Standing Alexandered – "Form" arm movements and **cross-pattern stepping**: front one, back to center, back one, back to center, side one, back to center, side two, back to center, while counting from 1 – 20, back to 1. End at "center" prior to extending and lowering arms.

4. *Cross Pattern 2*: Standing Alexandered "form" arm movements and **cross-pattern stepping** while **speaking text**. End at "center" prior to extending and lowering arms.

5. *Form-style*: Standing Alexandered: **"dance"** movements while staying in form and **speaking text** while remaining Alexandered. End at "center" prior to extending and lowering arms.

6. *Free-form*: Standing Alexandered: **improvised** movements and speaking text while remaining Alexandered. End at "center" prior to extending and lowering arms.

•••

Forming our own style, based on learned methods, is what we all do every day of our lives. "What is the meaning of life?" my students sometimes respond when I ask if they have any questions at the end of studio or class. My straightforward answer to their witty question: "The meaning of life is to survive with style."

14

SCENEWORK & INSTRUCTIONAL REHEARSAL STEPS

STEPS: INSTRUCTIONAL (REHEARSAL)

1. DRAMATIC SCENE

2. WILDE/COWARD SCENE

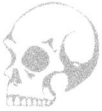

3. SHAKESPEAREAN MONOLOGUE

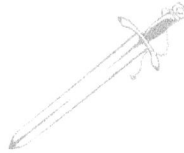

4. SHAKESPEAREAN SCENE

5. COMEDY SCENE

6. MOLIERE SCENE

7. COMMEDIA DELL' ARTE SCENE

8. CHEKHOV SCENE

SEQUENCE OF INSTRUCTIONAL (REHEARSAL) STEPS for
AMERICAN DRAMATIC SCENE

<u>First class</u>

1. CHAIR WORK – (sit, facing scene partner)
    * speak lines with eye contact (use script)
    * breathe in when listening

2. MAKE DEMANDS – for one minute, no pauses, make quick, brief
    demands of each other, back and forth ('I demand that you ....' 'I
    demand that you ...')
    * first, as actors
    * again, as characters

3. PARAPHRASE – Stand, facing each other and improvisationally
    paraphrase the scene (no scripts in hand).

<u>Second class</u>

4. INNER MONOLOGUE – DIALOGUE – (sit, facing scene partner)
    Volunteer actor speaks impulse subtext before you speak your line.

5. GIVEN CIRCUMSTANCE PREP – Each character claims
    environment/space; actor drops into character with 10-second deep
    breath prior to starting.

Third class

6. SOUND & MOVEMENT – Actors "gibberish-and-sound-speak" the
    scene while moving improvisationally.

7. EXPLORE SPACE: Invade, Conversational, Long Distance
    * invade character's space on a line
    * create conversational space on another line
    * place distance between you on another line or phrase (improvise)

8. MAKE CHOICES (in preparation for **second round**)
    * choose a psychological gesture
    * choose a character "meaningful object" for you and scene
    * make voice, speech, physicality choices based on your character
    profile paper

OSCAR WILDE or NOEL COWARD SCENE

Preparation: Cut scene 6-8 minutes max.

To prepare for first round: **1)** Chair work **2)** Share research with your partner **3)** Practice British or Received Pronunciation **4)** Work space-explo-
ration with your partner **5)** Make spatial and movement choices, so when
you present your first round you will have the scene on its feet and moving.
**This will be the only unit of work that Joe will be "directing," in order
to concentrate on the acting styles of the periods.**

SEQUENCE OF INSTRUCTIONAL (REHEARSAL) STEPS for
SHAKESPEAREAN MONOLOGUE
ROUND ONE: (Each Actor works individually)

1. SCANSION AND TARGETING

2. PRONUNCIATION AND MEANING

3. PAUSE/CATCH-BREATH AT END OF EVERY 10 SYLLABLE
    BLANK VERSE LINE

4. FULL STOP AT PERIODS AND COLONS: Works best when using
    original folio

5. SPEAK THE MEANING: Catch-breaths and full breaths only to
    support meaning without breaking the rhythm of the meter.

6. VERSE & MOVEMENT: Releasing meaning and language via the
    body (similar to a simple sound and movement exercise, but with blank
    verse text).

In the second round presentations of their monologues they are provided written notes from all three instructors: acting, voice/speech, and
movement, prior to their third, and final, round performance.

•••

After the monologue work the actors should explore Shakespearean scenes; the actors should be encouraged, if not expected, to work on their own scansion, targeting, pronunciation, meaning, and verse work, prior to their first round presentation of their scene on book with scripts in hand.

SEQUENCE OF INSTRUCTIONAL (REHEARSAL) STEPS for **SHAKESPEAREAN SCENEWORK**

LECTURE & EXPLORATION DAY:

5. Each scene explores scansion/prose language, pronunciation and meaning.
6. Each scene explores breaking at the end of every ten syllable line.
7. Each scene explores full stops and periods and colons.
8. Each scene explores what it is to SPEAK THE MEANING: Catch-breaths and full breaths only to support meaning without breaking the rhythm of the meter.

ROUND ONE: (Each actor works individually, then with partner)

1. ACT THE MEANING: Catch breaths and full breaths—only to support meaning without breaking the rhythm of the meter

2. **WORDZZ** & MOVEMENT: Releasing meaning and language out the body – with the help of two volunteers (*the next scene to go up*) feeding the words to actors as they work.

3. AFFECT YOUR PARTNER: with wordzz and movement and Imagery – send soundz through your body to your partner, make note of rhythms/patterns

4. SUBTEXT WITH PARTNER: Volunteers – Inner monologue/ dialogue – images – with the help of two volunteers (*the next scene to go up*) – the volunteers feed images/impulse responses to actors as they work through the scene.

ROUND TWO:
Evaluated on paper by profs (and notes from class) on the following:
Scansion
Emotional commitment
Character development
Voice
Character movement
Character profile paper
Progress on challenges and/or acting problems
Language use: communication of text, speech, meaning, pronunciation
Synthesis of internal process and external technique
Progress on achieving character profile goals

ROUND THREE: (Final Round - All actors perform on the dame day)
All evaluated, based on round two assessment categories

SEQUENCE OF INSTRUCTIONAL (REHEARSAL) STEPS for
CLASSIC COMEDY SCENE

First class

1. CHAIR WORK – (sit, facing scene partner)

    * speak lines with eye contact (use script)

    * breathe in when listening

2. MAKE DEMANDS – for one minute, no pauses, make quick, brief demands of each other, back and forth ('I demand that you ....' 'I demand that you ...')

    * first, as actors

    * again, as characters

Second class

3. TIMING WITH SPACE (each step done with a section of the scene or entire scene, as time allows)

    * pause before your line

    * seamless cues

    * movement after your line, partner cannot speak until your movement has stopped

    * synthesize all three into the scene

Third class

4. TIMING WITH PING-PONG 'N' PAUSE (with "bean bags" and text) (See Chapter Five for details)

Fourth class

5. EXPLORE SPACE: Invade, conversational, long distance

    * invade character's space on a line

    * create conversational space on another line

    * place distance between you on another line or phrase (improvise)

6. TRANSITIONS (from beat-to-beat or unit-to-unit)

Fifth class

7. WHISPER & INCREASE-SPEED-THRU

    Whisper the scene from beginning to end, increasing the urgency and speed, as you progress through the scene.

8. MAKE GENUINE CHOICES

    * choose a psychological gesture

    * choose a character "meaningful object" for you and/or the scene

    * make voice, speech, physicality choices based on your character profile paper

SEQUENCE OF INSTRUCTIONAL (REHEARSAL) STEPS for
MOLIÈRE SCENE

Lecture and Exploration Day: with scripts in hand

1. CHAIR WORK – (sit, facing scene partner)

    * speak lines with eye contact (use script)

    * breathe in when listening

<u>Second class</u>

2. MOVE ON EVERY LINE (a portion of the scene)
    Moving improvisationally, use gestures, cross, sit, stand, in any
    combination.

3. CROSS / MOVE <u>AFTER</u> YOUR LINE (another portion of the scene)
    CROSS / MOVE <u>BEFORE</u> YOUR LINE (another portion of the
    scene)
    CHOOSE FROM ALL THREE (mix & match with entire scene)
    *(have 2 minutes' worth of scene MEMORIZED for our next class)

<u>Third class</u>

4. BALLET/OPERINA: move through scene as if in a ballet and sing as
    if performing opera *
    * (have 2 minutes' worth of scene MEMORIZED for this step)

5. TIMING WITH PING-PONG 'N' PAUSE (with "bean bags" and
    text)
    (See Chapter Five for details)

<u>Fourth class</u>

6. WHISPER & <u>INCREASE-SPEED</u>-THRU
    Whisper the scene from beginning to end, increasing the urgency and
    speed, as you progress through the scene.

7. MAKE GENUINE CHOICES
    * choose a psychological gesture
    * choose a character "meaningful object" for you and/or the scene
    * make voice, speech, physicality choices based on your character
    profile paper

SEQUENCE OF INSTRUCTIONAL (REHEARSAL) STEPS for
COMMEDIA DELL'ARTE SCENE

Lecture and Exploration Day: with scripts and/or textbooks in hand
Discuss commedia stock character detailed descriptions in textbook.
Explore commedia stock characters: stance/walk/voice.

First class:
1. TIMING WITH PING-PONG 'N' PAUSE (with "bean bags" and text)
   (See Chapter Five for details)

2. CONTINUOUS SOUND (Moment before, between lines, during "silent" actions; sound always)

Second class:
3. MOVE ON EVERY LINE (a portion of the scene)
   Moving improvisationally, use gestures, cross, sit, stand, in any combination
   CROSS / MOVE AFTER YOUR LINE (another portion of the scene)
   CROSS / MOVE BEFORE YOUR LINE (another portion of the scene)
   CHOOSE FROM ALL THREE (mix & match with entire scene)

4. BALLET/OPERINA: move through scene as if in a ballet and sing as if performing opera *
   * (have 2-minutes worth of scene MEMORIZED for this step)

Third class:

5. ADD 1 CHARACTER LAZZI and 2 SCENE LAZZIS
    (See Chapter Five for details)

6. POSING – Pose at the end of each "phrase," then synthesize and
    moderate into scene.

Rehearsal Prep for Second Rounds

7. WHISPER & <u>INCREASE-SPEED</u>-THRU
    Whisper the scene from beginning to end, increasing the urgency and
    speed, as you progress through the scene.

SEQUENCE OF INSTRUCTIONAL (REHEARSAL) STEPS for
CHEKHOV SCENE

First class:

1. **THE HUMAN ELEMENT**:
    CHAIR WORK: "drop-in" the words, keep eye contact
    *For **emotional depth** (stay connected to serious/dramatic aspects)
    CHAIR WORK: "drop-in" the words, keep eye contact
    *For **comedic kernel** (stay connected to comedic aspects of exact same
    lines)
    (These are repeat steps with pairings, after introducing today in class.)
    *(This is THE HUMAN ELEMENT: comedy and drama in each moment
    and/or phrase.)*

2. BALLET/OPERINA: move through scene as if in a ballet and sing as if performing opera *
   * (have 2-minutes worth of scene MEMORIZED for this step)
   *(After Ballet/Operina exercise, ask the following: What's the scene about? Who am I? What do I want?)

Second class:

3. **SUBTEXT, PROPS AND ACTION**
   *(use props and space- positive & negative - as an "emotional prop")
   *(Use props every time you speak and when you engage in silent action.)
   *(An all-class exercise after introducing today.)
   *(Bring 2 props or choose 2 props for next class.)

Third class:

4. **THE PSYCHOLOGICAL "GESTURE"** – and/or voice, speech, walk, movement
   * choose a psychological gesture
   * choose a character "meaningful object" for you and scene
   * make voice, speech, and physicality choices, based on your character profile paper

Fourth class:

5. **THE HEART OF THE CHARACTER** – From where in the body does the character emanate? This will bring you closer to **The Human Element**: Comedy and Drama in each moment and/or phrase while communicating as the character.

15

CASTING, THE DAILY WARM UP, AND STAYING POSITIVE

Even if you do not consider yourself a director, you will be casting scenes in the studio or classroom. If you are a director, you already know that every new directorial assignment presents unique challenges; it is never, ever "the same as before." What *can* remain consistent is your attitude and your approach to every project; this will affect the casting process more than any appropriate research and preparation. As the saying goes: *it starts at the top.* You set the pace, you create the working environment, and you are the arbiter of style, design, and casting. I mention design here because you will be responsible for presenting your designers and production team with a concept for the production. Should you not be fortunate enough to have a "team," you still need a concept prior to casting. Pretend that you do have a design and production team as you formulate your concept; go for the ideal, with a limitless budget, no holds barred. This concept will be the basis for your casting process. Familiarizing yourself with the ideal cast will allow you to think on your feet and "on the fly" during the actual casting process. A concept will give you the freedom to know how far you can compromise or what adjustments will be needed. It will also give you the added advantage to recognize how hidden strengths in the actors could make up for not having the ideal actor in the role. Don't begin the casting process with what you do not have; begin with what you want or think you need.

The days prior to casting auditions, re-read the script and list the pivotal scenes that demand specific skills. I create a casting chart or Excel matrix and include these scenes or special skills with the roles that need to be kept in mind. And, as difficult as it might be for the called-back actors, I include the pivotal scenes in the list of callback scenes; most of the time, I'm impressed by the innovations the actors utilize to address the demanding scenes. It is rare that I have cast a play or musical the way I intended prior to auditions after observing callbacks. The actors inevitably pull me in a different direction during the callback process and this merges with my concept. So, for those of you who are not blessed with designers and a production team, here is where you, as directors, have an advantage because you do not have to rigidly stick to your previously devised concept. If a production and design team is already working away on your initial concept, it can be challenging to allow for innovations to merge with your previously devised concept, if the innovations affect the designs and build. If you work with designers and a production team that allow for the casting and rehearsal process to inform the final product, consider yourself one very lucky artist; you are the exception and should build on this blessing; build your program or theatre around this artistic gift. I'm serious. Market this rarity, build on it and spread the news. Yes ... they will come.

One of the things I've learned, most of the time the hard way, is that you must cast the actors who will work with you. Once I learned this, I never turned back. I cast actors who I know will work with me, even if they are not the most talented. Life's too short. I do not cast actors who do not listen or are living in an old re-run movie in their heads that no one can reach. I know my casting confounds people, especially the people who think I'm pretty good at what I do. They don't get it, and that's fine.

Cast for maximum impact on the audience. I direct for the audience; therefore, I cast for the audience, who, for obvious reasons, cannot be present for the casting. I direct actors in a manner that consistently reminds them that they are not performing for themselves; I remind them that they must tell the story to and for the audience. I have known artists I truly admire and respect who can perform for no one, no audience, and be perfectly content, or who prefer to ignore the audience; I understand this meditation. I see it as just that – meditation. But the audience pays good money to be included, to be a vital, final "missing piece" in this thing called live theatre. The audience will know who you are before you even have the time to introduce your art. The boss you think is your boss is not your boss; the audience is your boss. Cast for maximum impact on the audience. They will thank you.

Make friends with the stereotype and work with it. If you cast the stereotype, do it and be creative with it. If you cast against type, have the actor work with the stereotypical characteristics. And, by the way, if you are casting against type, the audience should be able to recognize the reason. Don't do it just to do it; the audience wants to be included; give them a reason and they will most likely appreciate it.

Warm up your actors or have them get in the habit of warming up as a group or individually prior to rehearsals and performances. In the studio, I utilize a ten-minute warm-up at the start of my novice acting classes; I use this warm-up prior to each rehearsal but we usually don't have time to stick to it, so I've learned that the actors actually prefer to come up with their own "cast warm-up," one they devise as a group. This is actually better for the cast, believe it or not, because it is something they "own." It's theirs, so they are likely to make it something special, something that keeps them bonded to each other throughout the rehearsal process and performance run. As the director, you're the creative boss, but you don't need to control everything. Give your actors some space. A warm-up that they devise for themselves is healthy for them and you. (My simple but extensive ten-minute warm-up is in the Appendix, should you be interested.)

It seems, at times, that staying positive is the answer to all paths to success. Self-help books and motivational speakers often include this on their lists for success (or, specifically, for success in achieving their particular goals). As clichéd as this may seem, there is a reason why staying positive works. For one, it's not negative; and, as humans, we seem to respond better to positive reinforcement, whether it comes from an expert, a boss, a colleague, a mentor, or ourselves. Yes, there is some truth to the notion that humans absolutely respond to fear. Some teachers believe that "fear is the greatest motivator." And we all understand why fear would, and does, motivate. Meeting the deadlines; losing out; getting the deal closed; failing the test; keeping up with social expectations; holding up the process; letting our colleagues down; not meeting our self-imposed goals. These motivating factors hold power over us; they are weighty. Some of them increased your blood pressure just a bit, as you read them, because you know the feeling oh, so well. But we needn't be over-burdened by fear. Why? Because it's everywhere; it's everywhere we look, every day of our lives. Fear is primal. But hope saves us. So what have we got to lose by staying positive? Maybe we'll live longer.

•••

Take genuine risks based on who you are and what you know. If the risks are "successful" – whatever that means to you – great – if no one seems to like your risks, rest assured that you will have grown as an artist. If it's never a waste of time for actors to take risks, the same goes for you as a mentor and director.

•••

Make decisions and stick to them – they will lead you to innovative results, if you listen to yourself and allow for some flexibility.

•••

Follow your gut and don't second-guess yourself.

APPENDIX

BREATH, MOVEMENT, AND APPLICATION

The actor-training process is a contractual agreement: the student pays to be trained; the professor or instructor is paid to train. It's a contract. And actors in training deserve to have their feedback in writing. Oral critiques are all well and good, but they are not firm; oral feedback is too flimsy and cannot hold the student actor and the instructor to their word. Written feedback carries weight, there are consequences, and it demands attention from the student actor. It also requires and implies that the professor or instructor is as clear as possible about what is being asked of the actor. What *exactly*, *specifically* does the actor need to address to progress or meet the studio challenge? And in an arts school, college or university setting, written feedback creates a positive, inclusive and fair grading environment, grading not left to the whims, moods, and personality of the instructor or student actor, but rather based on the instructor's artistic philosophy and pedagogical goals. It is good for all involved. And, yes, it takes a bit of effort and paper, but I believe it is a key factor to actor-training success.

Actors must learn how to address notes from instructors, coaches, and directors. If the teacher or coach provides proper feedback in writing, the actor should be expected to take note and address it immediately. This involves translating the note into image and incorporating that image into action. This depends on the actor's ability to imagine, *to see* the expected result in her or his mind. People without imaginations, who cannot visualize, cannot address notes in a timely fashion. And if they cannot address notes, they have no business on any professional stage, sound stage, or studio. This actor must go back to square one and find out why he or she cannot visualize. This will be rare in graduate school and beyond. It is, however, quite common in undergraduate and high school age actors.

The following pages contain different types of evaluation forms. They range from freshman (college level) evaluations to BFA acting studio evaluation forms. Also included is the previously mentioned ten-minute warmup; it consists of these type of exercises: aerobic breathing; martial art; power breathing; muscle stretch; joint and vocal release; neck release; and spinal stretch.

EVALUATION FORMS

BFA ACTING STUDIO

Ole Miss Theatre
Cantu

PROCESS MONOLOGUE
2nd Round Notes

NAME:_____

| Under-rehearsed | Min. Improvement | Improvement | General Progress | Exceptional Progress |
| 5 (21-22) | 6 (23-24) | 7 (25-26) | 8 (27-28) | 9-10 (29-30) |

Given Circumstance Prep
Voice
Speech
Character Physicality
Character Believability
Character Profile Paper
Preparation of all assignments
Process Monologue Assignment - 30% weight: (Studio actor, please list goals from 1st Round here, prior to 2nd Round.)
Completed Character Profile Paper is due at 2nd Round Presentation

COMMENTS:

BFA ACTING STUDIO   Ole Miss Theatre
                                                Cantu

PROCESS MONOLOGUE
Final Round Evaluation

NAME:_____

No Improvement   Min. Improvement   Good Work   Considerable Progress   Exceptional Progress
   5 (21-22)   6 (23-24)   7 (25-26)   8 (27-28)   9-10 (29-30)

	No Improvement	Minimal Improvement	Good Work	Considerable Progress	Exceptional Progress
Given Circumstance Prep					
Voice					
Speech					
Character Physicality					
Character Believability					
Character Profile Paper					
Preparation of all assignments					
Process Monologue Assignment (30 % weight): (Please list 1st Round goals, in pencil or pen, here)					
POINTS					

COMMENTS:

_____

Total Points: _____   Grade _____

BFA ACTING STUDIO   **Ole Miss Theatre**
                                         Cantu

TWO-MINUTE AUDITION
1st Round Notes

NAME:_____

Under-rehearsed	Poor	Good	Very Good	Exceptional Work
5	6	7 8 -9		10

First Monologue   Choice of Material:
                         Voice & Speech:
                         Movement:
                         Character Work:

Second Monologue   Choice of Material:
                         Voice & Speech:
                         Movement:
                         Character Work:

Audition Skill:
2-Minute Limit (based on actual time):
ADDITIONAL COMMENTS:

BFA ACTING STUDIO   **Ole Miss Theatre**
                                         Cantu

TWO-MINUTE AUDITION
Final Round Evaluation

NAME_____

Under-rehearsed	Poor	Good	Very Good	Exceptional Work
5	6	7 8 -9		10

First Monologue   Choice of Material:
                         Voice & Speech:
                         Movement:
                         Character Work:

Second Monologue   Choice of Material:
                         Voice & Speech:
                         Movement:
                         Character Work:

Audition Skill:
2-Minute Limit (based on actual time):
ADDITIONAL COMMENTS:

BFA ACTING STUDIO **Ole Miss Theatre**
  Cantu

TWO-MINUTE AUDITION

NAME:_____

No Improvement	Min. Improvement	Good Work	Very Good Work	Exceptional Work
5	6	7	8 - 9	10

First Monologue:

Choice of Material	5	6	7	8	9	10
Voice & Speech	5	6	7	8	9	10
Movement	5	6	7	8	9	10
Character Work	5	6	7	8	9	10

Second Monologue:

Choice of Material	5	6	7	8	9	10
Voice & Speech	5	6	7	8	9	10
Movement	5	6	7	8	9	10
Character Work	5	6	7	8	9	10

Audition Skill	5	6	7	8	9	10
2-Minute Limit: ___	5	6	7	8	9	10

COMMENTS:

_____

Total Points: _____   Grade _____

BFA ACTING STUDIO　　　　　　　　**Ole Miss Theatre**
　　　　　　　　　　　　　　　　　　　Cantu

CLASSIC AMERICAN DRAMATIC SCENE
2nd Round Notes

NAME:_____ Scene:_____

Under-rehearsed	Min. Improvement	Improvement	General Progress	Considerable Progress
5	6	7	8	9 - 10

Given Circumstance Prep
Character Development
Listening, Responding, Working with Partner
Voice
Speech
Character Physicality
Progress: On Challenges and/or Acting Problems
Communication of Text/Subtext
Character Profile Paper
Preparation of all assigned steps

COMMENTS:

BFA ACTING STUDIO   Ole Miss Theatre
                                         Cantu

CLASSIC AMERICAN DRAMATIC SCENE
Final Round Evaluation

NAME:_____ Scene:_____

No Improvement   Min. Improvement   Good Work   Considerable Progress   Exceptional Progress
       5   6   7   8   9 - 10

	No Improvement	Minimal Improvement	Good Work	Considerable Progress	Exceptional Progress
Given Circumstance Prep					
Character Development					
Listening, Responding, Working with Partner					
Voice					
Speech					
Character Physicality					
Progress: On Challenges and/or Acting Problems					
Communication of Text/Subtext					
Character Profile Paper					
Preparation of all assigned steps					
TOTAL POINTS					

COMMENTS:

_____

Total Points: _____   Grade _____

BFA ACTING STUDIO

Ole Miss Theatre
Cantu

CLASSIC COMEDY SCENE
2nd Round Notes

NAME:_____ Scene:_____

Under-rehearsed	Min. Improvement	Improvement	General Progress	Considerable Progress
5	6	7	8	9 - 10

Given Circumstance Prep
Comedic Character Development/Honest Choices
Listening, Responding, Working with Partner
Voice
Speech
Character Physicality
Progress: On Challenges and/or Acting Problems
Character Profile Paper
Comedic Values / Technique / Transitions
Preparation of all assigned steps

COMMENTS:

BFA ACTING STUDIO   **Ole Miss Theatre**
                                          Cantu

CLASSIC COMEDY SCENE
Final Round Evaluation

NAME:_____ Scene:_____

No Improvement	Min. Improvement	Good Work	Considerable Progress	Exceptional Progress
5	6	7	8	9 - 10

	Under-rehearsed	Minimal Improvement	Good Work	Considerable Progress	Exceptional Progress
Given Circumstance Prep					
Comedic Character Development/Honest Choices					
Listening, Responding, Working with Partner					
Voice					
Speech					
Character Physicality					
Progress: On Challenges and/or Acting Problems					
Character Profile Paper					
Comedic Values / Technique / Transitions					
Preparation of all assigned steps					
TOTAL POINTS					

COMMENTS:

_____

Total Points: _____   Grade _____

BFA ACTING STUDIO   **Ole Miss Theatre**
                                          Cantu

WILDE/COWARD SCENE
2nd Round Notes

NAME:_____ Scene:_____

Under-rehearsed	No. Improvement	Min. Improvement	Improvement	Considerable Progress
6	7	8	9	10

Rhythm & Pace of Scene
Character Development
Comedic Values / Style
Voice
Language Use: meaning, text communication; dialect (speech)
Character Movement
Progress: On Challenges and/or Acting Problems
Synthesis: Internal Process / External Technique
Character Profile Paper
Progress on Achieving Profile Goals

COMMENTS:

BFA ACTING STUDIO   **Ole Miss Theatre**
                                         Cantu

WILDE/COWARD SCENE
Final Round Evaluation

NAME:_____ Scene:_____

No Improvement	Min. Improvement	Good Work	Very Good Work	Exceptional Progress
6	7	8	9	10

	No Improvement	Minimal Improvement	Good Work	Very Good Work	Exceptional Progress
Rhythm & Pace of Scene					
Character Development					
Comedic Values/Style					
Voice					
Language Use: meaning; text communication; dialect (speech)					
Character Physicality					
Progress: On Challenges and/or Acting Problems					
Synthesis: Internal Process/ External Technique					
Character Profile Paper					
Progress On Achieving Profile Goals					
TOTAL POINTS					

COMMENTS:

_____

Total Points: _____   Grade _____

BFA ACTING STUDIO

Ole Miss Theatre
Cantu

FINAL PROJECT: SHAKESPEARE SCENE
2nd Round Notes

NAME:_____ Scene:_____

No Improvement	Min. Improvement	Good Work	Very Good Work	Exceptional Progress
6	7	8	9	10

Scansion
Character Development
Emotional Commitment
Voice
Language Use: Speech, Interpretation, Text Communication
Character Physicality
Progress: On Challenges and/or Acting Problems
Synthesis: Internal Process / External Technique
Character Profile Paper
Progress on Achieving Profile Goals

COMMENTS:

BFA ACTING STUDIO

**Ole Miss Theatre
Cantu**

FINAL PROJECT: SHAKESPEARE SCENE
Final Round Evaluation

NAME:_____ Scene:_____

No Improvement	Min. Improvement	Good Work	Very Good Work	Exceptional Work
6	7	8	9	10

	No Improvement	Minimal Improvement	Good Work	Very Good Work	Exceptional Work
Scansion					
Character Development					
Emotional Commitment					
Voice					
Language Use: Speech; Interpretation; Text Communication					
Character Physicality					
Progress: On Challenges and/or Acting Problems					
Synthesis: Internal Process/External Technique					
Character Profile Paper					
Progress On Achieving Profile Goals					
TOTAL POINTS					

COMMENTS:

_____

Total Points: _____   Grade _____

BFA ACTING STUDIO **Ole Miss Theatre**
                      Cantu

MOLIÈRE SCENE
2nd Round Notes

NAME:_____ Scene:_____

Under-rehearsed	Min. Improvement	Improvement	General Progress	Considerable Progress
5	6	7	8 - 9	10

Honest Impulse
Comedic Character Development
Listening, Responding, Working with Partner
Voice
Speech
Character/Styles: Movement
Progress: On Challenges and/or Acting Problems
Character Profile Paper
Comedic/Moliere Styles Technique
Progress On Achieving Character Profile Goals

COMMENTS:

BFA ACTING STUDIO

Ole Miss Theatre
Cantu

MOLIÈRE SCENE
Final Round Evaluation

NAME:_____ Scene:_____

Under-rehearsed	Min. Improvement	Good Work	Considerable Progress	Exceptional Work
5	6	7	8 - 9	10

	5	6	7	8 - 9	10
Honest Impulse					
Comedic Character Development					
Listening, Responding, Working with Partner					
Voice					
Speech					
Character/Styles: Movement					
Progress: On Challenges and/or Acting Problems					
Character Profile Paper					
Comedic/Moliere Styles Technique					
Progress On Achieving Character Profile Goals					
TOTAL POINTS					

COMMENTS:

_____

Total Points: _____   Grade _____

BFA ACTING STUDIO

Ole Miss Theatre
Cantu

COMMEDIA DELL'ARTE SCENE
2nd Round Notes

NAME:_____ Scene:_____

Under-rehearsed	Min. Improvement	Improvement	General Progress	Considerable Progress
5	6	7 - 8	9	10

Lazzi
Commedia Character Development
Listening, Responding, Working with Partner
Voice
Speech
Character/Styles: Physicality
Progress: On Challenges and/or Acting Problems
Character Profile Paper
Commedia Styles Technique
Progress On Achieving Character Profile Goals

COMMENTS:

BFA ACTING STUDIO   **Ole Miss Theatre**
                                         Cantu

COMMEDIA DELL'ARTE SCENE
Final Round Evaluation

NAME:_____ Scene:_____

Under-rehearsed	Min. Improvement	Good Work	Considerable Progress	Exceptional Work
5	6	7 - 8	9	10

	5	6	7 - 8	9	10
Lazzi					
Commedia Character Development					
Listening, Responding, Working with Partner					
Voice					
Speech					
Character/Styles: Physicality					
Progress: On Challenges and/or Acting Problems					
Character Profile Paper					
Commedia Styles Technique					
Progress On Achieving Character Profile Goals					
TOTAL POINTS					

COMMENTS:

_____

Total Points: _____   Grade _____

BFA ACTING STUDIO   **Ole Miss Theatre**
                                         Cantu

CHEKHOV SCENE
2nd Round Notes

NAME:_____ Scene:_____

Under-rehearsed	Min. Improvement	Improvement	General Progress	Considerable Progress
5	6	7 - 8	9	10

Subtext, Props, and Action
Character Development
Listening, Responding, Working with Partner
Voice
Speech
Character/Styles: Physicality
Progress: On Challenges and/or Acting Problems
Character Profile Paper
Chekhov Styles Technique: Human Element - Comedy & Drama & Breath
Progress On Achieving Character Profile Goals

COMMENTS:

BFA ACTING STUDIO   Ole Miss Theatre
                                         Cantu

CHEKHOV SCENE
Final Round Evaluation

NAME:_____ Scene:_____

Under-rehearsed	Min. Improvement	Good Work	Considerable Progress	Exceptional Work
5	6	7 - 8	9	10

	5	6	7 - 8	9	10
Subtext, Props, and Action					
Character Development					
Listening, Responding, Working with Partner					
Voice					
Speech					
Character/Styles: Physicality					
Progress: On Challenges and/or Acting Problems					
Character Profile Paper					
Chekhov Styles Technique: Human Element - Comedy & Drama & Breath					
Progress On Achieving Character Profile Goals					
TOTAL POINTS					

COMMENTS:

_____

Total Points: _____   Grade _____

THEA 110
Freshman Performance Studies

Ole Miss Theatre
Cantu

TWO-MINUTE ACTIVITY/
CONTEMPORARY MONOLOGUE
Second Round Notes

NAME:_____

Under-rehearsed	No Improvement	Some Improvement	Improvement	Greatly Improved
5	7	9	11	12/13

Preparation/Time	5	7	9	11	12
Focus/Timing	5	7	9	11	13
Creating/Responding To Environment	5	7	9	11	13
Character Development/ Physicality	5	7	9	11	12
Activity	5	7	9	11	12
Honest Impulse	5	7	9	11	13
Character Profile Paper	5	7	9	11	13
Achieving Profile Goals	5	7	9	11	12

COMMENTS:

_____

Total Points: _____   Grade _____

THEA 110   **Ole Miss Theatre**
Freshman Performance Studies   **Cantu**

TWO-MINUTE ACTIVITY/
CONTEMPORARY MONOLOGUE
Final Round

NAME:_____

Under-rehearsed/ Digressed	Min. Improvement	Good Work	Very Good Work	Exceptional Work
5	7	9	11	12/13

Preparation/Time	5	7	9	11	12
Focus/Timing	5	7	9	11	13
Creating/Responding To Environment	5	7	9	11	13
Character Development/ Physicality	5	7	9	11	12
Activity	5	7	9	11	12
Honest Impulse	5	7	9	11	13
Character Profile Paper	5	7	9	11	13
Achieving Profile Goals	5	7	9	11	12

COMMENTS:

_____

Total Points: _____   Grade _____

THEA 110
Freshman Performance Studies

Ole Miss Theatre
Cantu

SCRIPT ANALYSIS

PLAY TITLE: _____

FROM SYLLABUS:
SCRIPT ANALYSIS: 3 PLAYS
You must choose **three** plays to analyze: a Greek Classic *from the required textbook anthology*, an Early or Mid-Twentieth Century Drama *from the required textbook anthology* and an Ethnic or Non-traditional Contemporary play (with professor's approval) or Contemporary Drama *from the required textbook anthology*. Write a minimum 5-page **typewritten paper, 12 point Arial font, double-spaced,** containing: 1) synopsis; 2) character breakdown; 3) plot structure analysis; 4) a one-page list of published dramatic criticism or scholarly reviews of the play, minimum of three quoted sources; and a 5) personal response to the analysis of the play. You will also prepare a **5-minute** (timed) **oral report** based on your analysis of the play. You will need to turn in your paper when you deliver your oral presentation. You may not do your oral presentation unless you are also turning in your paper. *Class will complete their presentations for Greek before presenting on 20th Century, etc.* Five points off if you do not present when scheduled; **five points off for late papers.**

NAME: _____

Paper

5-page min. typewritten, 12 pt., Arial, dbl-spcd or 1.5 (**10 points**)   _____

Synopsis (**15 points**)   _____

Plot structure analysis (**10 points**)   _____

Character Breakdown (**15 points**)   _____

One-page report of published
dramatic criticism or scholarly
reviews (**20 points**)   _____

Personal response to
the analysis of the play (**5 points**)   _____

Oral Report

Content (**15 points**)   _____

Presentation (**10 points**)   _____

COMMENTS:

Total Points _____   Grade _____

THEA 110   Ole Miss Theatre
Freshman Performance Studies   Cantu

TWO-MINUTE AUDITION
1st Round

NAME:_____

Under-rehearsed	Minimal Improvement	Average Work	Good Work	Very Good Work	Exceptional Work
5	6	7	8	9	10

First Monologue:

Choice of Material	5	6	7	8	9	10
Voice & Speech	5	6	7	8	9	10
Character Development	5	6	7	8	9	10

Second Monologue:

Choice of Material	5	6	7	8	9	10
Voice & Speech	5	6	7	8	9	10
Character Development	5	6	7	8	9	10

Movement/Physicality	5	6	7	8	9	10
Honest Impulse	5	6	7	8	9	10
Audition Skill	5	6	7	8	9	10
2-Minute Limit: ___	5	6	7	8	9	10

COMMENTS:

Total Points _____   Grade _____

THEA 110
Freshman Performance Studies

Ole Miss Theatre
Cantu

TWO-MINUTE AUDITION
Final Round

NAME:_____

Under-rehearsed	Minimal Improvement	Average Work	Good Work	Very Good Work	Exceptional Work
5	6	7	8	9	10

First Monologue:

Choice of Material	5	6	7	8	9	10
Voice & Speech	5	6	7	8	9	10
Character Development	5	6	7	8	9	10

Second Monologue:

Choice of Material	5	6	7	8	9	10
Voice & Speech	5	6	7	8	9	10
Character Development	5	6	7	8	9	10

Movement/Physicality	5	6	7	8	9	10
Honest Impulse	5	6	7	8	9	10
Audition Skill	5	6	7	8	9	10
2-Minute Limit: ___	5	6	7	8	9	10

COMMENTS:

Total Points _____   Grade _____

THEA 110   **Ole Miss Theatre**
Freshman Performance Studies   **Cantu**

CONTEMPORARY COMEDY SCENE
2nd Round Notes

NAME:_____

Under-rehearsed 8	Min. Improvement 9	Progress 10	Substantial Progress 11	Exceptional Progress 12/13

Focus/Timing	8	9	10	11	12
Moment Before/ Honest Impulse	8	9	10	11	12
Voice/Speech	8	9	10	11	12
Physicality/ Use of Space	8	9	10	11	13
Character Development	8	9	10	11	13
Listening/Responding/ Working with Partner	8	9	10	11	13
Character Profile *(based on paper)*	8	9	10	11	13
Character Profile *(from 1st round)*	8	9	10	11	12

COMMENTS:

_____

Total Points: _____   Grade _____

THEA 110
Freshman Performance Studies

Ole Miss Theatre
Cantu

CONTEMPORARY COMEDY SCENE
Final Round

NAME:_____

Under-rehearsed	Min. Improvement	Gen. Progress	Substantial Progress	Exceptional Work
8	9	10	11	12/13

Focus/Timing	8	9	10	11	12
Moment Before/ Honest Impulse	8	9	10	11	12
Voice/Speech	8	9	10	11	12
Physicality/ Use of Space	8	9	10	11	13
Character Development	8	9	10	11	13
Listening/Responding/ Working with Partner	8	9	10	11	13
Character Profile	8	9	10	11	13
Character Profile (from 2nd round)	8	9	10	11	12

COMMENTS:

_____

Total Points: _____   Grade _____

THEA 169
Freshman Voice and Movement

Ole Miss Theatre
Cantu

30% of Course Grade
ALEXANDER TECHNIQUE/STANDARD AMERICAN ACTIVITY MONOLOGUE
1st Round

NAME:_____

	No Improvement 6/12	Min. Improvement 7/14	Good Work 8/16	Very Good Work 9/18	Exceptional Work 10/20
Activity	12	14	16	18	20
Alexander Technique	12	14	16	18	20
Standard American Speech	12	14	16	18	20
Voice	6	7	8	9	10
Character Profile Paper	6	7	8	9	10
Achieving Profile Goals	6	7	8	9	10
Length of Monologue (3 - 5 minutes)	6	7	8	9	10

COMMENTS:

Total Points: _____   Grade _____

THEA 169
Freshman Voice and Movement

Ole Miss Theatre
Cantu

30% of Course Grade
ALEXANDER TECHNIQUE/STANDARD
AMERICAN ACTIVITY MONOLOGUE
2nd Round

NAME:_____

No Improvement	Min. Improvement	Good Work	Very Good Work	Exceptional Work
6/12	7/14	8/16	9/18	10/20

Activity (20%)	12	14	16	18	20
Alexander Technique (20%)	12	14	16	18	20
Standard American Speech (20%)	12	14	16	18	20
Voice	6	7	8	9	10
Character Profile Paper	6	7	8	9	10
Achieving Profile Goals	6	7	8	9	10
Length of Monologue (3 - 5 minutes)	6	7	8	9	10

COMMENTS:

Total Points: _____   Grade _____

THEA 169　　　　　　　　　　　　　**Ole Miss Theatre**
Freshman Voice and Movement　　　　**Cantu**

30% of Course Grade
ALEXANDER TECHNIQUE/STANDARD
AMERICAN ACTIVITY MONOLOGUE
Final Round

NAME:_____

No Improvement 6/12	Min. Improvement 7/14	Good Work 8/16	Very Good Work 9/18	Exceptional Work 10/20

Activity (20%)	12	14	16	18	20
Alexander Technique (20%)	12	14	16	18	20
Standard American Speech (20%)	12	14	16	18	20
Voice	6	7	8	9	10
Character Profile Paper	6	7	8	9	10
Achieving Profile Goals	6	7	8	9	10
Length of Monologue (3 - 5 minutes)	6	7	8	9	10

COMMENTS:

_____

Total Points: _____　　Grade _____

10-MINUTE WARM UP

Picking Grapes

Centering Exercise

4-Corner Breathing

Neck Rolls / Stretches

The Blossom

Head Bowl Stretch

Neck Clasp

The Hula

Arm Curls

The Puppet (drop/stack)

This warm-up consists of these type of exercises: aerobic breathing; martial art; breathing; muscle stretch; joint & vocal release; neck release; spinal stretch; and ends with aerobic breathing and vocal release.

•••

Consistent and accurate feedback will produce lasting results.

BIBLIOGRAPHY

1) http://www.comm.unt.edu/histofperf/tiffanyvandewall/Charlotte.html. 2001. The University of North Texas.

2) Stanislavski, Constantin, *An Actor Prepares*. reprint. Routledge, 1989.

3) Stanislavski, Constantin, *Building a Character*. Bloomsbury Revelations. 2013.

4) Stanislavski, Constantin, *Creating a Role*. Bloomsbury Revelations. 2013.

5) Spolin, Viola, *Improvisation for the Theatre*, Northwestern University Press.

6) Cohen, Robert, *Acting Professionally*, Mayfield Press.

7) Rudlin, John, *Commedia dell' Arte: An Actor's Handbook*, Routledge Publishing.

8) Wilbur, Richard/ Jean Baptiste Poquelin De Molière, *Tartuffe*, Harvest/HBJ Publishers.

9) Schmidt, Paul/Chekhov, Anton, *The Plays of Anton Chekhov*, Harper Collins.

10) Krause, Alvina. Forever Beginning, [article] by Alvina Krause, North western Tri-quarterly, Fall 1962.

11) Maupin, Elizabeth. Finding the comedy in Chekhov: Mad Cow Theatre sets out to demystify the Russian playwright by comparing his 'Seagull' to—among other things—'Survivor. [article] The Orlando Sentinel (Orlando, FL). March 11, 2007.

12)   Linklater, Kristin. *Freeing The Natural Voice*, Drama Publishers.

13)   Eleanor Margolies, editor. *Theatre Materials: What is theatre made of?*
       Published by Centre for Excellence in Training for Theatre/Central
       School of Speech and Drama.

14)   Olivieri, Joseph. *Shakespeare Without Fear*. Harcourt College
       Publishers, Orlando, Florida. 2001.

15)   VASTA. Voice and Speech Trainers Association. www.vasta.org

16)   Laban Contemporary Dance. www.laban.org.

17)   Gray, John. *The Alexander Technique*. St. Martin's Press, New York.
       1991.

18)   The International Jacques Lecoq Theatre School.
       www.ecolejacqueslecoq.com/jacques_lecoq

19)   Skinner, Edith. *Speak With Distinction*. Applause: Theatre Book
       Publishers, New York. 1990.

20)   Hagen, Uta. *Respect For Acting*. Wiley Publishing, Inc. New York.
       1973.

21)   American Theatre magazine (published by the Theatre Communications
       Group.) January 2010.

22)   IPA Phonetic symbols. Type. http://ipa.typeit.org/.

23)   King, Hilary. Alexander Technique.
       http://www.hilaryking.net/glossary/end-gaining.html

ABOUT THE AUTHOR

Joe Turner Cantu

An actor trainer, playwright, and director, Joe is a theatre professor and head of the acting program in the Department of Theatre Arts at The University of Mississippi (Ole Miss), and for ten years was artistic director of Oxford Shakespeare Festival. His teaching expertise is in acting process, acting styles, and directing. Joe has also taught at The University of Texas at Austin, The University of Michigan in Ann Arbor, Northern Arizona University and at his alma mater, Southern Methodist University, where he earned his BFA in Theatre and MFA in Acting. In 1972, Joe was the proud recipient of the Samuel French Award, Best Performer in the State of Texas (4-A high schools.)

In the late 1980s, Joe was recipient of a Rockefeller Playwright in Residence grant for his play, *Rock and Betty Dance*. During this time, he was an associate artistic director at Stages Repertory Theatre in Houston, Texas. Joe has directed across the USA and in Peru. In April 2008, Joe performed in a Ping Chong and Company production of *Secred Histories: Oxford*. Joe is a member of The Dramatists Guild, Inc. In 2006, Joe was the recipient of the Cora Lee Graham Award (Outstanding Teacher of Freshmen), awarded by the College of Liberal Arts at The University of Mississippi. In 2015, Joe was awarded a Senior Summer Research Grant by the College of Liberal Arts in support of his playwriting. Joe and his husband, Eddie Upton, live and work in Oxford, Mississippi.

ACKNOWLEDGEMENTS

I thank my teachers and mentors: Jack Clay, Jim Hancock, Margaret Loft, Dale A.J. Rose, Raymond Caldwell, Dennis Holt, Kristin Linklater, Tina Packer, and Ted Swindley. I thank my former and current students, from whom I learn daily. I thank my former students who provided sample character profiles. I thank my former and current colleagues, particularly Jennifer Mizenko, Brian Evans, Rory Ledbetter, and Rene Pulliam. A very special thank you goes to Virginia's best friend, Cheryl Frankfater, whose edits helped me breathe new life into the book. I thank The University of Mississippi, particularly the College of Liberal Arts, for research and sabbatical support. Thank you, Neil White, for believing in me and my work. And thank you, Eddie Upton, for never letting me give up on all our dreams.